THE RIGHTS OF
THE CRITICALLY ILL

An American Civil Liberties Union Handbook

THE RIGHTS OF THE CRITICALLY ILL

JOHN A. ROBERTSON

THE BASIC ACLU GUIDE TO THE RIGHTS OF
CRITICALLY ILL AND DYING PATIENTS

General Editor:
NORMAN DORSEN,
President, ACLU

BALLINGER PUBLISHING COMPANY
Cambridge, Massachusetts
A Subsidiary of Harper & Row, Publishers, Inc.

International Standard Book Number: 0-88410-733-7

Library of Congress Catalog Card Number: 83-3789

Printed in the United States of America

Library of Congress Cataloging in Publication Data

Robertson, John A. (John Ancona)
  The rights of the critically ill.

  (An American Civil Liberties Union handbook)
  Includes bibliographical references and index.
  1. Critically ill—Legal status, laws, etc.—United States.
2. Terminally ill—Legal status, laws. etc.—United States. I. Title.
II. Series. [DNLM: 1. Critical care—Legislation. 2. Ethics, Medical.
3. Patient advocacy. 4. Terminal care—Legislation. W 85 R651r]
  KF3823.R63   1983   344.73'0419   83-3789
  ISBN 0-88410-733-7   347.304419

For Alice B. Rutkowski,
who first introduced me to these issues

"Caius is a man, men are mortal, therefore Caius is
mortal," had always seemed to him correct as applied
to Caius, but certainly not as applied to himself.
That Caius—man in the abstract—was mortal,
was perfectly correct, but he was not Caius, not an abstract
man, but a creature quite, quite separate
from all others. He had been little Vanya, with a
mamma and a papa, with Mitya and Volodya, with the
toys, a coachman and a nurse, afterwards with
Katenka and with all the joys, griefs, and delights
of childhood, boyhood, and youth. . . . Caius really was mortal,
and it was right for him to die; but for me, little Vanya, Ivan
Ilych, with all my thoughts and emotions, it's altogether
a different matter. It cannot be that I ought
to die . . . It can't be. It's impossible! But here it
is. How is this? How is one to understand it?"

—Tolstoy: *The Death of Ivan Ilych*

Acknowledgments

This book could not have been written without the warm support and assistance of several people. Dr. Norman Fost and Professor Daniel Wikler, colleagues in the University of Wisconsin Medical School's Program in Medical Ethics, unstintedly gave intellectual and emotional support. I am particularly grateful for their patience and incisive discussion of many of the issues addressed herein, and for Norman's sharp editorial eye. I also owe an enormous debt to George Annas, who first steered me into this field, provided comfort and insight all along the way, and gave me the immediate impetus for writing this book. For thorough and dedicated research I am extremely grateful to Debora Kennedy and Alison Karlsson, who provided essential assistance at important stages of this project, and to Paula Cochran who enabled it to be finished. Joann Lynne and Alan Weisbard kindly read earlier drafts and prevented me from making several errors. Finally, I have been very fortunate to have been part of the Law School and Program in Medical Ethics of the University of Wisconsin. They provided the supportive atmosphere that made this book possible.

Contents

Preface

This guide sets forth your rights under the present law, and offers suggestions on how they can be protected. It is one of a continuing series of handbooks published in cooperation with the American Civil Liberties Union (ACLU).

Surrounding these publications is the hope that Americans, informed of their rights, will be encouraged to exercise them. Through their exercise, rights are given life. If they are rarely used, they may be forgotten and violations may become routine.

This guide offers no assurances that your rights will be respected. The laws may change and, in some of the subjects covered in these pages, they change quite rapidly. An effort has been made to note those parts of the law where movement is taking place, but it is not always possible to predict accurately when the law *will* change.

Even if the laws remain the same, their interpretations by courts and administrative officials often vary. In a federal system such as ours, there is a built-in problem since state and federal law differ, not to speak of the confusion between states. In addition, there are wide variations in the ways in which particular courts and administrative officials will interpret the same law at any given moment.

If you encounter what you consider to be a specific abuse of your rights, you should seek legal assistance. There are a number of agencies that may help you, among them, ACLU affiliate offices, but bear in mind that the ACLU is a limited-purpose organization. In many communities, there are federally funded legal service offices which provide assistance to persons who cannot afford the costs of legal representation. In general, the rights that the ACLU defends are freedom of inquiry and expression; due process of law; equal protection of the laws; and privacy. The authors in this series have discussed other rights (even though they sometimes fall outside the ACLU's usual concern) in order to provide as much guidance as possible.

These books have been planned as guides for the people directly affected; therefore, the question and answer format. (In some areas there are more detailed works available for "experts.") These guides seek to raise the major issues and inform the nonspecialist of the basic law on the subject. The authors of these books are themselves specialists who understand the need for information at "street level."

If you encounter a specific legal problem in an area discussed in one of these handbooks, show the book to your attorney. Of course, he or she will not be able to rely exclusively on the handbook to provide you with adequate representation. But if your attorney hasn't had a great deal of experience in the specific area, the handbook can provide helpful suggestions on how to proceed.

Norman Dorsen, President
American Civil Liberties Union

The principal purpose of this handbook, as well as others in this series, is to inform individuals of their legal rights. The authors from time to time suggest what the law should be, but their personal views are not necessarily those of the ACLU. For the ACLU's position on the issues discussed in this handbook, the reader should write to Librarian, ACLU, 132 West 43 Street, New York, NY 10036.

Introduction

Critical illness is a difficult time for patients, their families, and health-care providers. Life and death hang in a delicate balance. Adding to the stress is medical and legal uncertainty about the effect of decisions to start, continue, or stop treatment.

This book describes the legal rights and duties of patients, families, and health-care providers, in situations of critical illness. Its primary purpose is to help the participants understand the legal implications of their decisions. Since the law generally gives priority to the patient's interests, the book focuses on critical illness from the patient's perspective, rather than from the perspective of the family, health-care providers, or the state. Since patient rights define by implication, the rights and duties of those interacting with him, the book also provides an account of the rights and duties of the family, doctors, nurses, and the state, as well as the rights of critically ill patients.

Given the legal uncertainty that surrounds these decisions, legal knowledge of legal rights has significance for all parties involved. It is important for patients and families who encounter insensitive or hostile medical personnel. It is important for medical people who want to know the limits of their authority, so that they may protect their patients, respect their rights, and avoid legal liability. Knowledge of the law is also crucial to the lawyers, judges, and legislators who resolve disputes and enact the laws affecting the treatment of the critically ill.

The term *critically ill* is used to cover patients who, if not treated, will die in the immediate future, or suffer some long-term harm. It includes newborns, children, adults, and the elderly. In some cases, treatment will restore the patient to a state of normal health. In other instances, treatment will not "cure" illness, but will blunt its worst effects, or alleviate a crisis. In still other cases, treatment will merely postpone for days, weeks, or months, an impending and inevitable death.

As used in this book, a right is the legitimate claim or entitlement that someone else provide an individual with a service or resource (a positive right)—providing treatment— or not interfere with his decision to use or refuse a service or resource (a negative right)—refusing surgery. That "someone else" could be the family, doctors, nurses, the hospital, or even the state. The rights discussed here are legal rights because they are backed by the force of law. If called upon, the courts will recognize them and use the power of the state to enforce them.

Some people consider discussions of legal rights in situations of critical illness as legalism carried to an extreme. Can legal rights matter to very ill persons close to death, or to the families, doctors, and nurses who must deal with the stresses and indignities of dying? The assumption of this book is that in many important ways, they can. At stake are decisions about life and death, and the well-being of patients and families in some of the most trying circumstances they will ever face. These decisions have enormous personal and social significance for patients, their families, and physicians, as well as on the allocation of medical resources.

The need for attention to legal rights becomes obvious when we recognize the conflicts of interest that may arise in critical illness. In any situation of critical illness there are several parties with different and often conflicting interests and perspectives. The patient, the family, the doctors, the nurses, the hospital, and the public, all have something at stake in the decisions made about the critically ill. While they may have common interests in some cases, their interests often diverge or conflict. The patient, for example, may be ready to die and want no further treatment. The family, however, may want the person to stay alive because of deep love and concern, unresolved guilt feelings, or religious scruples. Or, public officials may feel that such a decision constitutes suicide. In other situations, the patient, though disabled or debilitated, may want to keep fighting to eke out every possible second of life, while the family, worn out by stress and strain, or motivated by resentment or financial interests, might hope that the patient dies and try to influence care accordingly.

Central figures in these dramas will be the doctors and nurses treating the patient, who bring their own value preferences to bear on any decisions they might make. They may be professionally motivated to use their medical skills whenever possible to keep people alive, resulting in highly intrusive and expensive medical treatments that may run counter to the needs of the patient and her family. Or, they may feel that further treatment is pointless because of the patient's hopeless condition, even though the patient and his family view the matter differently. In some cases, they may find treatment to be so stressful, that there will be an unstated reluctance to do anything further. This will influence what patients and families are told, and the care that is actually given.

The continuation of treatment, disclosure, and experimentation—the important decisions that persons face in situations of critical illness—are legally protected. Doctors, in particular, may find that this emphasis on legal rights gives the book an adversarial tone which is inappropriate or unrealistic for the practice of medicine. Medicine often is, and should be, a trusting, cooperative venture among doctor, patient, and family. But all trusting relations depend upon a backdrop of rules to protect against an abuse of trust. That is the role of the legal rights discussed in this book.

Law, however, has its limits, and is no guarantee of the outcomes that we think desirable or morally required. One important limit in this context is that legal rights are often unclear or vaguely defined. The courts have faced only some of the conflicts that arise in the care of the critically ill, and even then, have not always dealt adequately with the full complexity of the dilemmas involved. Necessarily then, many of the rights described in this book are estimates or predictions of how the courts would rule if faced with a particular conflict, rather than descriptions of how they actually have ruled.

A second limit concerns the enforcement of these rights. The theoretical existence of a right, and its realization in practice, are two different things. The critically ill person is, if anything, at a disadvantage in this regard. As countless patients know, it is difficult for sick persons and their families to assert their rights in the health care system. Sick patients who find themselves in opposition to their families and doctors, will have an even more difficult time securing their rights. As a result, many of the rights described here might seem to be more honored in the breach, than in the observance. Closing the gap between rights and practice in the care of the critically ill is the goal of this book.

I

The Right to Know the Truth and Keeping Confidences

Critically ill patients, like other patients, have a need to be dealt with openly and honestly by their doctors. While some patients prefer to deny the seriousness of their illness, many others want assurances that their doctor is not hiding the truth from them. Patients may also want their illness to be a private affair, with its nature and details withheld from outsiders, including, in some cases, family members. This chapter discusses the patient's right to avoid or obtain information about his illness, and to keep it from others.

Does a person have a right to know if he has cancer or is terminally ill?

Yes, though this might be hard to enforce legally. Surveys invariably show that, contrary to the beliefs and practices of some doctors, most patients want to know the truth about their illnesses and their impending death.[1] Until recently, however, doctors often withheld this information from patients,[2] as a way to maintain hope and to protect the patient from the shock of reality. Instead, doctors often would tell the family, with both the family and doctor then carrying on an elaborate charade that the patient was actually getting better. Some commentators have suggested that this reluctance is caused by the physician's own discomfort in facing death, or his guilt in not being able to save a patient.

Recent surveys now show a substantial change in the disclosure practices of physicians.[3] The change is due to a greater awareness of patients' rights, and the availability of effective treatment for many forms of cancer. Physicians now find it

5

easier to discuss diagnosis and prognosis truthfully with their patients.

While no court has held a doctor liable for withholding or distorting relevant information, under general principles of tort law, a person in a fiduciary relation to another, could be held liable for such actions. As a matter of tort law, such information would be essential so that patients would be able to give informed consent to the therapy that the doctor recommends; a patient cannot decide whether to accept the risks of a proposed therapy over alternative courses of action (including doing nothing), without knowing the diagnosis and chances for recovery. The truth about diagnosis and prognosis is also relevant because of other decisions that a dying patient must face, concerning finances, work, and relations with family members and friends.

The right to be told the truth of one's illness could also exist as a matter of express or implied contract between doctor and patient. It would be a matter of express contract if the doctor had agreed to tell the full truth and then misled the patient. Courts could also find disclosure to be an implied term of the doctor-patient contract, on the theory that the patient consults the doctor, at least in part, for expert information on which to base future choices. Such a contract is likely to be implied if truthful disclosure becomes a more common medical practice than it has been in the past.

In many states patients now may enforce their right to know the truth of their illness by exercising their legal right to see their medical records.[4]

Can a doctor lie to a patient about diagnosis and prognosis to save the patient anxiety and grief?

Only if the patient has specifically said he does not want to be told the truth about his condition. If the patient has said that he wants to know, the doctor would be obligated to tell him as a matter of contract law, though if it were totally irrelevant to future medical, financial, or other decisions, the patient might not be able to collect any damages for breach of the contract.

If the patient has not specifically said anything one way or the other, the doctor could still be liable if the withheld information were relevant to the medical, financial, and personal decisions that the patient would face. Saving the patient from anxiety and grief is not sufficient justification for withholding information. The strongest case for withholding the truth would be if a doctor had reason to believe that the person would prefer not to know. Most surveys show that patients want this information, even though naturally, few welcome the news. In a rare instance, if the shock of the knowledge itself would injure the patient or render him incompetent, a therapeutic privilege to withhold information might be found.

Can a doctor be sued for telling the patient the truth about a fatal illness?

Only if the doctor acted maliciously and intentionally inflicted emotional distress by telling the patient information in a brutal or unfeeling way that deviated from disclosure practices among physicians, or if he should have known that the information itself would cause injury, or if he violated a specific request by a patient not to be told the truth. In general, however, patients who have not asked not to be told, could not very easily win suits against doctors for being told the truth about their illness. Indeed, doctors have won cases where they mistakenly told the patient that he was terminally ill when they had mistakenly, though nonnegligently, erred in their diagnosis.[5]

Does the patient have a right to be told the truth about her illness if the family objects?

Yes. The competent patient's right to know the truth about her illness cannot be waived or exercised by the family. Whether acting from humanitarian or selfish motives, the family has no right to control the information given a competent patient about her illness. Their wishes may unconsciously reflect their own fears or be attempts to manipulate the patient. Also, family members who have never discussed the question openly with the patient, may not know, or accurately reflect, the patient's wishes. Thus, doctors should not withhold the truth from a patient just because the family has asked the doctor to do so. Following their wishes, would be no defense to a suit by the patient, and the family could not sue the doctor for overriding their wishes.

However, the family's objection to disclosure would help the doctor in determining whether the truth would so injure the patient, that withholding it were justified. But in that case, the reason for nondisclosure would be the effect on the patient, not the family's wishes. The family has no right to have information about the patient, relevant to her situation, withheld from her.

Does a patient have a right to have information about his disease and prognosis withheld from his family or others?

Yes. The doctor-patient relationship is confidential. A doctor can be sued for disclosing personal information arising out of treatment without the patient's consent. Exceptions to the rule of confidentiality exist if information about a patient's disease is necessary to protect others from contagion, prevent crime, or avert some other substantial harm.[6] However, the general interest of the family has not been held to be one of those exceptions, and if done without the patient's consent, could breach the doctor's duty of confidentiality. Thus, a doctor could be successfully sued for telling the family or others details about a patient's illness, even if the patient had not specifically asked the doctor to keep it confidential.

As a practical matter, doctors often tell the family the diagnosis and prognosis—indeed, sometimes telling them, rather than the patient. If the patient has not specifically forbidden the doctor from telling his family, a doctor might be able to defend a suit for breach of confidentiality by relying on a theory of implied consent, or on the custom of telling the family, particularly when close family members need to plan and prepare for an impending death. However, this custom would be no defense if the patient had asked that the information be kept confidential. In no case should the doctor give outsiders information about the patient's diagnosis and prognosis without his consent.

Does a critically ill patient have a right of privacy?

Yes. The term *privacy*, as used legally, has two senses: (1) control of personal decisions, discussed in chapter IV, and (2) protection of a person's physical and mental solitude or seclusion. The latter or traditional sense of privacy also includes protection from the public disclosure of private facts protected by the rules of confidentiality.

It is clear that the critically ill patient's right of privacy in this second sense is legally protected, and damages can be awarded for its breach. For example, publication of photographs of a patient's body, without a patient's consent, even without her name, is actionable.[7] Also, unconsented intrusions on a patient's solitude or peace, may also invade her privacy. Medical or other hospital personnel not connected with her case, such as medical students, have no right to enter her hospital room if the patient objects. Nor can photographs be taken without the patient's consent. In one case, a surgeon who had previously treated a dying patient's neck cancer, came into his room and took pictures of the patient for his medical files. Since the patient objected, and the photographs were not a part of his treatment, the court allowed damages for invasion of privacy and assault and battery, even though there was no publication of the photographs, and it was done to promote science.[8]

Do family members have a right of privacy in a court hearing to stop treatment?

No. As will be discussed in chapters V and VII, family members who object to the further treatment of a very sick child, spouse, or other family member, may end up in a court hearing to determine whether treatment may legally be stopped. Such hearings add to the enormous stress of these decisions, and often are the object of intense media and public attention. There is no right to have such hearings closed, or the proceedings kept out of the public eye. Indeed, a law which ordered them to be closed, would be vulnerable to attack as interfering with the First-Amendment rights of free speech and free press.[9] However, it may be possible to close court hearings that involve the termination of treatment on children if they occur in juvenile court, since juvenile court proceedings traditionally have been closed to both the public and the press.

NOTES

1. Mitchell and Glicksman, *Cancer Patients: Knowledge and Attitudes*, 40 Cancer 61–66 (1977).
2. Oken, *What to Tell Cancer Patients: A Study of Medical Attitudes*, 175 J. Amer. Med. Assn. 1120–28 (1961).
3. Novack, Plumer, Smith, Oehitill, Morrow, and Bennett, *Changes in Physicians' Attitudes Toward Telling the Cancer Patient*, 241 J. Amer. Med. Assn. 897 (Mar. 2, 1979).
4. Annas, *The Rights of Hospital Patients*, 112–21 (1975).
5. Greinke v. Keese, 82 Misc. 2d 996, 371 N.Y.S. 2d 58 (1975). See also Kraus v. Spielberg, 37 Misc. 2d 519, 236 N.Y.S. 2d 143 (1962).

6. Annas, *The Rights of Hospital Patients*, 121–25 (1975); Horne v. Patton, 287 So. 2d 824 (Ala. 1973); Simonsen v. Swenson, 177 N.W. 831 (Neb. 1920).
7. Waltz and Inbau, *Medical Jurisprudence*, 271–74 (1971); Clayman v. Bernstein, 38 Pa. D&C 543 (1940).
8. Berthiaume's Estate v. Pratt, 365 A. 2d 797 (Me. 1976).
9. Richmond Newspapers, Inc. v. Virginia, 448 U.S. 761 (1980).

II

The Right to Treatment and Control of Medication

The competent patient's right of self-determination includes the right to have medical treatment, as well as to refuse it. Indeed, most critically ill persons will want medical treatment— as much of it as they can get.

In such cases, treatment will usually be offered. But conflicts between the patient and doctors and family over the type and extent of treatment may still occur. The patient may want more medical care than his family or the doctor are willing to provide. They may think the patient would be better off if death comes sooner, and may erroneously think that the patient agrees. Or, they may want treatment stopped because of its expense, because of fears of their own death, because of the turmoil and stress of caring for someone critically ill, or because of malice toward the patient.

More common, perhaps, are conflicts between the patient and doctor (with the family aligned with one or the other) over the exact methods of treatment. The patient may want information about his illness and prognosis that the doctor is unwilling to give. He may want treatments that conflict with the doctor's view of good medicine. Or, the patient might demand access to drugs that are controversial or illegal. This chapter deals with the right of the competent adult who is critically ill, to receive medical treatment, and his right to determine particular aspects of it.

Does a critically ill person have the right to be treated?
It depends. Since doctors are not obligated to treat everyone in need, he has no right to be treated. If a person is under the care of a doctor, and if treatment will benefit him,

11

the doctor is obligated to treat him as long as the patient wants treatment or until he notifies him of his unwillingness to treat in time for him to arrange for equivalent care with another doctor. The rule is that once the doctor has undertaken to treat a patient, he cannot abandon him.[1] Doctors whose abandonment causes injury, have often been sued for malpractice.

These rules apply to private as well as public hospitals. Hospitals are not obligated to admit and treat any patient, but once they do, they are obligated to treat the patient as long as treatment will help, or until alternative care can be arranged. In addition, if the private hospital maintains an emergency room, it has a legal duty to provide emergency care to all who need it, though it would not be obligated to admit patients to the hospital after such treatment.[2] It also has a legal duty to admit patients whose doctors have been given admitting privileges. Public or municipal hospitals are in a different situation and may be obligated to admit all patients.

Does a critically ill person have a right to be treated if he is unable to pay for the treatment?

It depends on a variety of factors. A complete discussion of who is responsible for the costs of critical illness and the extent to which patients who are unable to pay have a right to medical treatment is found in chapter XII, "Costs and Allocation of Scarce Resources."

See chapter XII for a more detailed discussion of the effect of costs on the patient's right to be treated.

Can the family stop treatment on a critically ill patient who wants it to be continued?

No. Spouses, parents, children, and other family members, have no legal power to prevent a competent patient who wants treatment, and has the resources to pay for it, from receiving it. (However, the family may refuse to pay for any further treatment that it is not legally obligated to provide.) This is true even if the care is costly and the patient is terminally ill. As long as continuation of treatment will benefit the patient, she has the right to be treated. In these situations the doctor's duty is to the patient, and not the family. If there is a conflict, he must follow the patient's wishes. If care were withheld against the patient's wishes and the patient died, the family members taking the action, and doctors and other medical staff implementing it, could be found civilly and criminally liable.

In cases of terminal or very critical illness, it may be unclear whether treatment must be provided to patients who demand it. However, the consenting patient has a right to have treatment that will lengthen survival by even a few days, even if it leaves the patient in a debilitated or weakened state. The right might be limited, however, if the patient insisted that she receive maximum treatment and be kept alive indefinitely in a comatose or unconscious state.

Does a critically ill patient have a right to very expensive or uncertain treatments that the doctor or family oppose?

It depends. The patient has a right to receive the best care available that is reasonably likely to help him. Thus, the doctor has an obligation to offer the patient very expensive treatments if they have a reasonable chance of prolonging the patient's life or curing his illness. If the doctor opposes treatment that a substantial minority of doctors use, she is obligated to inform the patient so that the patient could seek treatment from them. However, if the treatment will provide little benefit to the patient, and is not used by a respectable minority of doctors, she may have no obligation to offer it, or even inform the patient of its availability elsewhere.

The family has no right to prevent the patient from receiving treatments that might help him, though they are not obligated to pay for them. This is true even if they are so expensive that they will eat up any possible inheritance from the patient and not significantly prolong the patient's life. A competent adult may spend his money on expensive medical care if he chooses, and the family cannot legally stop him. They might claim that he is incompetent and try to control the care he receives. But incompetency does not automatically give them rights over the patient's care. A doctor in this situation should do what the patient wants, and if there are doubts about his competency, seek to have a guardian appointed.

Does a competent person have the right to determine the extent and type of medical care he will receive once he becomes incompetent and no longer able to decide?

Probably. In states with "living will" laws (see chapter VIII) a person may be able to specify the types of treatment, if any, that he wants to receive once he becomes incompetent. If the directive is binding, as it is in some states, the doctor and the family may not be able to withhold or give certain additional care as they choose. If the patient has given such a directive, a treatment that would benefit the patient cannot be withheld on the ground that the patient would now want care stopped if competent to state his preference. However, the doctor and family would not be obligated to provide expensive or uncertain treatments beyond that which is required for incompetent patients just because the patient so directed when he was competent. Directives for care when incompetent only assure that the patient receives beneficial treatment he is otherwise legally entitled to receive. The doctor and the family are not obligated to satisfy every wish made in the directive.

Does a patient have a right to receive palliative care if she has rejected life-saving care?

It depends. Patients who reject treatments that their doctors think are essential, may still want medical care. Sometimes doctors will refuse to treat such patients. This problem arises frequently with cancer patients who reject their doctor's recommendations for surgery, radiation, and/or chemotherapy. Rather than undergo the rigors of treatment, they sometimes refuse treatment and accept an inevitable death. However, they may still want to stay under their doctor's care and receive palliative care.

If the doctor notifies the patient of his refusal to treat her on these terms in time for the patient to find another doctor, his refusal would not constitute abandonment.

If there's no time to arrange alternative care, the patient's right to continue to be treated by his doctor—and the doctor's right not to treat him further—is unclear. According to several Jehovah's Witness cases,[3] the doctor is not obligated to undertake a course of treatment that would amount to medical malpractice, such as removing a ruptured spleen without blood transfusions. It is not clear, however, whether these statements would control if an alternative source of care were not available, and the doctor's refusal to perform the surgery would cause death. The courts are likely to compel the doctor to provide the limited care that the patient wants, even if this runs counter to his medical judgment until a doctor willing to treat the patient on his terms, can be found.

The informed consent of a competent adult to receive less than full care, should relieve the doctor of liability for treating the patient in a way that would otherwise lead to a charge of malpractice.

Thus, cancer patients who reject their doctor's recommendations probably have forfeited their right to have their doctor continue treatment. There is usually time to find another doctor, and the doctor's refusal may not deny them life-prolonging therapy. Many physicians will not abandon patients who make such difficult decisions, but they can legally refuse to give further care.

Does a patient have the right to receive effective medication for pain?

Probably not. Once a doctor accepts a patient, she is obligated to provide him with the best treatment customarily provided by other doctors. This would include treatment for pain. A doctor who failed to live up to the standard of care of other doctors for pain relief, could be civilly liable. However, doctors have traditionally failed to alleviate pain.[4]

As more attention is paid to the effective management of chronic pain, by combining several drugs and administering them on a preventive, rather than on an "as needed" schedule, a medical standard of care assuring critically ill patients effective pain relief, may be established. In that case, a doctor treating a terminally ill cancer patient who is unaware of the preventive pain relief used by many cancer experts, could be liable for negligently caused pain and suffering. However, unless the doctor has also been negligent in other aspects of the treatment, it is unlikely that suits for negligent undermedication alone will be brought, since the potential damages are not great, and in some jurisdictions may not be recognized at all. The only remedy available might be for the patient to discuss with his doctor his attitudes, beliefs, and knowledge about pain and its relief. If the doctor's statements are not satisfactory, the patient might choose another doctor; otherwise, the doctor would be obligated, as a matter of contract, to provide the methods of pain relief promised.

Does a critically ill patient have the right to determine the drugs that will be used in his treatment?

Yes and no. He must give a free, informed consent for the administration of drugs. Drugs cannot be forced on him against his will. Since a competent adult patient may reject care, he may also reject drugs that the doctor offers.

If the patient requests a drug that is legally available, and reflects good medical practice, he has the right to receive the drug from his doctor. However, he would be free to terminate care, and seek the drug from another doctor, if his request is refused on medical grounds.

What is the legal status of laetrile?

Laetrile, or amgydalin, is a derivative of apricot pits that, some persons claim, without scientific basis, to be an effective cure for cancer. This claim has generated hopes among thousands of cancer patients, ignited a political controversy about excessive government intervention in private matters, and produced a highly successful "legalize laetrile" movement at the state level. Government-sponsored experimentation on the effectiveness of laetrile was undertaken by cancer researchers at the Mayo Clinic. This study found laetrile to have "no substantive benefit in terms of cure, improvement, or stabilization of cancer . . . or extension of life span." It also found that it produced blood cyanide levels approaching lethal range. It concluded that "amygdalin (laetrile) is a toxic drug that is not effective as a cancer treatment."[5]

While there is overwhelming evidence that the promotion of laetrile as a cure for cancer involves self-deception, exploitation, and quackery, its use involves a basic issue of personal autonomy—the right of a patient to control his medical care. Its use also poses a dilemma for doctors caring for patients who irrationally believe in laetrile's efficacy, and who might reject conventional therapy if not also provided with laetrile. For these reasons it deserves discussion in this chapter.

Federal Law

Federal law does not specifically prohibit the use, possession, or prescription of laetrile, as it does heroin, marijuana, and other drugs. However, under the federal Food, Drug, and Cosmetic Act, laetrile cannot be imported or transported across state lines, because it has not been established as safe and effective.[6] (The act does not apply to the manufacture, sale, and distribution within a state.)

Proponents of laetrile have argued that the federal law does

not apply to laetrile, and that if it does, it violates the constitutional right of both the patient and his doctor to decide on
treatment.[7] They have won some lower court decisions on
both grounds.[8] In fact, a federal district court[9] has ruled in a
class action that terminally ill patients for whom conventional
therapy offered no hope, had a constitutional right to import
or receive laetrile. Under this decision, the government has
allowed patients with an affidavit from their doctor stating
that they are terminally ill, to import a three-month supply of
laetrile for their own use.

The United States Supreme Court decision in *United States
v. Rutherford,*[10] is likely to change this situation. In that
case, the court held that the Food, Drug, and Cosmetic Act
applies to drugs such as laetrile, used by the terminally ill,
and sent the case back to the lower court to decide its
constitutionality. The court, on remand, then held that the act
did not violate a terminally ill patient's right of privacy, and
was constitutional,[11] and the Supreme Court denied further
review.

State Law

State law on laetrile varies greatly and is rapidly changing
because of legislation and court decisions. A few states specifically forbid its manufacture, sale, or use by doctors,[12] though
not its possession or use by patients. While these laws could
be challenged as a violation of the patient's constitutional
right of privacy, particularly with regard to terminally ill
cancer patients or patients who are using laetrile to supplement standard therapy, laetrile proponents have had little
success in state courts. A New Jersey appellate court has held
that the prescription of laetrile does not constitute grounds
for denying a doctor hospital staff privileges.[13] However, the
California Supreme Court in *People v. Privatera,*[14] has held
that criminal penalties can be imposed on doctors who administer laetrile to cancer patients, even in the absence of fraud
and misrepresentation. It rejected the argument that the
constitutional right of privacy includes the right to obtain
unapproved drugs such as laetrile, from a willing doctor.
Although other states could rule differently on the matter, it
is likely that *Privatera* will be followed elsewhere.

Until recently, however, most states were silent on the

matter of laetrile, leaving its legal status unclear. Seventeen states have recently enacted legislation to clarify its legal status and to make laetrile available to patients who so desire it.[14A]

The details of state laetrile laws vary widely. Under most laws a doctor is not subject to criminal or civil liability or sanctions by the medical licensing board solely for prescribing laetrile to patients who request it.[15] Many of them specifically legalize the manufacture, distribution, sale, prescription, and administration of laetrile within the state, sometimes adding reporting and record-keeping requirements.[16] Some of the laws state that hospitals cannot prohibit the use of laetrile, or take away hospital privileges from doctors who prescribe or administer it.[17] In a few states the legal authorization for laetrile may be limited if a state board finds that it is harmful.[18] Surprisingly, only Louisiana and Texas restrict the use of laetrile to cancer patients[19] and only Illinois restricts its use to patients diagnosed as having terminal cancer— "cancer with a high and predictable mortality . . . (that) will probably result in death in a relatively short period of time."[20] Eight states [21] specifically require that the patients give written informed consent; it is usually necessary for the patient to submit a form in which he recognizes that laetrile is not a cure. This is to be filed then with a state board. The following request form from Indiana is typical:

WRITTEN INFORMED REQUEST
FOR PRESCRIPTION OF AMYGDALIN
(LAETRILE) FOR MEDICAL TREATMENT

Patient's name _____
Address _____
Age _____ Sex _____
Name and address of prescribing physician: _____

Malignancy, disease, illness or physical condition diagnosed for medical treatment by amygdalin (laetrile) or its use as a dietary supplement: _____

My physician has explained to me:
(a) That the manufacture and distribution of amygdalin (laetrile) has been banned by the Federal Food and Drug Administration.

(b) That neither the American Cancer Society, the American Medical Association, nor the Indiana State Medical Association recommend use of amygdalin (laetrile) in the treatment of any malignancy, disease, illness or physical condition.

(c) That there are alternative recognized treatments for the malignancy, disease, illness or physical condition from which I suffer which he has offered to provide for me including (Here describe).

_____

That notwithstanding the foregoing, I hereby request prescription and use of amygdalin (laetrile) (a) in the medical treatment of the malignancy, disease, illness or physical condition from which I suffer [ ], or (b) as a dietary supplement [ ] (check (a) or (b)).

Patient or person signing for patient

ATTEST:

_____

Prescribing physician

A copy of such "written informed request" shall be forwarded forthwith after execution thereof to the state board of medical registration and examination for appropriate filing.

The effect of these laws is to prevent a doctor from being civilly liable or subject to disciplinary sanctions solely because he has prescribed laetrile. However, they do not prevent the ordinary laws of malpractice, fraud, and informed consent, from operating. Doctors may still be subject to a loss of license, restriction of hospital staff privileges, and suits for damages, if they give laetrile without informing patients of its untested status and the availability of other therapies, or if they oversell or misrepresent its efficacy. While some people would argue that substituting laetrile for conventional therapy is malpractice even if the patient has consented, a successful suit is unlikely if the doctor has been honest and the patient has freely consented to its use.

In states without any legislation on laetrile, doctors could probably prescribe laetrile without being criminally or civilly liable if they had not misrepresented its status, and the patient had given a fully informed consent. However, professional sanctions could still be imposed by medical societies, licensing boards, or hospitals for giving laetrile when other therapies are available. Also ordinary rules of malpractice and consent would still apply.

Does a cancer patient have the right to have her doctor prescribe or administer laetrile?

No. Even in a state where doctors are legally permitted to prescribe laetrile to an informed patient, they are not obligated to do so. This is true whether or not the patient is terminally ill, and whether or not laetrile is being used as a supplement to, rather than a substitute for, conventional therapy. Since laetrile has not been shown to be effective, a doctor who refuses to prescribe it would not be violating his duty to provide the patient with effective medical care. If the patient objects, she is free to terminate the relationship and seek care elsewhere.

If the doctor agrees to use laetrile, the patient has a right to receive it only in those states that have not banned the drug, or if the criteria of any federal court order allowing its importation, is satisfied. Where laetrile is legally available under state law, it is available whether it is being used as a supplement to, or a substitute for, standard therapy, and whether or not the patient is terminally ill. (The exception is Illinois, where patients are required to be terminally ill in order to use laetrile.)[22]

Since state laws allowing doctors to treat patients with laetrile do not necessarily offer protection against subsequent claims of malpractice or unprofessional conduct, using laetrile as a supplement, rather than as an alternative to conventional therapy, will be preferable. Very high doses, however, could be toxic and thereby constitute negligence.[23] Doctors who give laetrile as a supplement to standard therapy are also less likely to be found guilty of unprofessional conduct by medical examining boards and hospitals. Doctors whose patients request laetrile should thus try to get the patient to agree to laetrile as a supplement, and not as a substitute for, standard therapy.

Does a terminally ill patient have the right to use heroin to relieve pain?

Not at the present time. Under the federal Controlled Substances Act and its state counterparts, heroin is classified as a drug without any valid therapeutic use.[24] Despite evidence that heroin is an effective painkiller and may have special advantages for some cancer patients, doctors may not prescribe or administer heroin.

The total ban on medical uses of heroin is unique to the United States. Many Western nations, including Great Britain and West Germany, permit heroin to be medically prescribed for the relief of pain. Many doctors in those countries find it to be more therapeutic than morphine and other opiates for certain patients and use it widely, either alone, or in a mixture with other drugs to relieve the pain associated with advanced or terminal cancer.[25]

One researcher who studied the effects of heroin in terminal patients at St. Christopher's Hospice in London, has found that heroin does not lead to impairment of mental faculties, does not require increasing dosages, or induce uncontrollable physical dependence, and has particular advantages because of its greater solubility with water.[26] Since heroin is two to four times as potent as morphine when injected, smaller and less frequent injections would be necessary. As a result of such studies, there is now considerable evidence that heroin is safer in clinical practice than earlier believed, and may be the drug of choice for patients who cannot tolerate large injections. However, some doctors disagree and do not think that there is any particular need for heroin.[26A]

As information of the British experience has reached America, many people concerned about the plight of cancer patients have argued that heroin be made available for the relief of terminal pain. The American Medical Association, as well as many state and local medical societies, have recommended that doctors be able to prescribe heroin. Legislation has been introduced in Congress and in several states,[27] and a petition has been filed under the Controlled Substances Act asking the Department of Justice to reschedule heroin to permit its medical use with dying patients.

Although the federal government has shown some response to these demands by setting up an inter-agency committee to study the matter, and funding studies through the National

Cancer Institute on heroin's pain-killing properties and efficacy relative to morphine, any change in the law is unlikely in the near future. The irrational fears that have characterized the U.S. policy toward heroin, the prejudices many doctors have about narcotics, the opposition of law enforcement agencies, and uncertainty about whether heroin is more effective, are probably too strong to overcome, despite evidence that some terminally ill patients would benefit.

A potentially more effective route to the legal availability of heroin than legislation or administrative action, is litigation. Although no test case has yet been brought, terminal patients may have a constitutional right to use heroin to relieve pain unmanageable by other drugs.[28] This right would derive from an extension of the constitutional right of privacy to personal decisions concerning medical care. If the patient has a constitutional right to decline necessary medical care (including in the eyes of some courts, the right to use laetrile when terminally ill), he may also have a right to choose a form of therapy that may be the most effective way to control chronic pain. Indeed, the case is stronger for a right to use heroin than laetrile, at least for a minority of patients for whom it may be the most effective way to get adequate pain relief. Unlike laetrile, its efficacy is not in doubt, and its use does not apparently deter patients from more effective therapies.

If a terminal patient's choice of pain medications such as heroin is recognized as an aspect of the fundamental constitutional right of privacy, the state would be hard pressed to show a compelling need for prohibiting its medical use. Possible addiction would not apply, since patients using it would be terminal, and the addictive potential is probably no greater than that of morphine. The risk of diversion into illicit channels would also be a weak argument, since strict regulation and reporting, as is now required for narcotics, would minimize this. Thus, there are strong constitutional arguments that terminal patients should not be denied heroin for the relief of cancer pain.

Does a critically ill patient have the right to use marijuana to relieve the side effects of chemotherapy?

It depends on the state. Recent studies have shown that marijuana might reduce the nausea and vomiting associated with cancer chemotherapy.[29] Like heroin and LSD, however, it has no recognized medical use under federal- and state-controlled substances laws,[30] and cannot legally be prescribed or used for the relief of the side effects of chemotherapy.

Recently, thirty-two states[31] have passed laws to allow marijuana to be prescribed or administered medically to treat glaucoma and the side effects of cancer chemotherapy. These laws remove state criminal liability from doctors who prescribe, and patients who use, marijuana for medical reasons. However, they have no effect on the illegal status of marijuana under federal law, and thus do not necessarily provide patients with a legal source of the drug.

Several of the states that allow the medical use of marijuana, have simply ignored this problem (Illinois, Oregon, and Nevada). New Mexico,[32] the first state to enact such legislation, has set a precedent for other states and made the medical use of marijuana lawful only as part of a state-run "controlled substances therapeutic research program." Under this scheme, a doctor who wishes to treat a patient with marijuana must first submit an application to a board of three doctors. The state officially functions as a researcher. It obtains the marijuana from the federal government and dispenses it to patients who have a prescription from a doctor participating in the research program. Initially, the federal bureaucracies involved made it very difficult to have marijuana released to these state programs. The National Cancer Institute now makes synthetic marijuana (THC) available for this purpose, but does not provide marijuana in smokable form, the form which many patients find most desirable to offset the nausea of chemotherapy. The federal barrier to the medical use of marijuana in smokable form thus remains.

Patients unable to obtain smokable marijuana for valid medical use might consider litigation. The same claim of a constitutional right to use medication to relieve pain as an aspect of privacy made with heroin, would apply, with the state's interest in regulating use even weaker, since marijuana is already widely available on the illegal market. As with heroin, the extent of the patient's right will depend on the alternatives available for controlling the side effects of chemotherapy, the burden placed on the patient by denial of the drug, and the state's interest in restricting the availability of marijuana.

Cancer patients who illegally use marijuana for the relief of nausea and vomiting associated with chemotherapy, might also have a defense of medical necessity[33] if prosecuted for growing or possessing the drug. They would have to show that no other drugs were available to control these side effects. Such a defense was recognized in a prosecution of a glaucoma victim for growing marijuana.[34] He had already lost much of his sight, and was able to demonstrate that marijuana was the only remedy available to prevent further deterioration of his vision. A cancer patient who did not respond to antivomiting drugs, but did to smokable marijuana, could also assert medical necessity as a defense.

Does a dying patient have the right to use LSD?

Not at the present time. A number of researchers[35] have found LSD to be potentially useful in helping terminal patients work through the denial, anger, and depression of impending death to achieve the acceptance that Kubler-Ross describes as the last stage of the dying process.[36] Like marijuana and heroin, however, LSD is not legally recognized as having any valid therapeutic use and cannot, at the present time, be prescribed under federal or state law.[37] Moreover, there is no strong lobby for its availability as there is with laetrile, marijuana, and heroin, and very little research is being conducted on its use with dying persons.

Both terminal patients and doctors treating them, could challenge laws prohibiting the use of LSD with dying patients. The right of dying patients to use LSD would seem to be part of the constitutional right of privacy and self-determination over medical care, as much as the use of laetrile, heroin, and marijuana. However, because there are alternatives to LSD for helping a patient to face and accept an impending death, the right to have LSD administered by a willing doctor might not be readily recognized as a right as in the case of heroin or marijuana.

NOTES

1. Waltz and Inbau, *Medical Jurisprudence*, 142–52 (1971).
2. Annas, *The Rights of Hospital Patients*, 37–44 (1975).
3. Application of President and Directors of Georgetown College, 331 F.2d 100 (D.C. Cir.), *cert. denied*, 377 U.S. 978 (1964); John F. Kennedy Memorial Hospital v. Heston, 58 N.J. 576, 279 A.2d 670 (1971).

4. J. Bonica, *The Management of Pain* (1953); *Relief of Intractable Pain*, 90, 222–25 (1974); Marks and Sachar, *Undertreatment of Medical Inpatients with Narcotic Analgesics*, 78 Annals Intern. Med. 173 (1973).

5. Moertel et al, *A Clinical Trial of Amygdalin (Laetrile) in the Treatment of Human Cancer*, 306, N. Eng. J. Med. 201 (Jan. 28, 1982).

6. 21 U.S.C. § 355.

7. F. Ingelfinger, *Laetrilomania*, 296, N. Eng. J. Med. 1167 (1977); Hodgson, *Restrictions on Unorthodox Health Treatments in California: A Legal and Economic Analysis*, 24 U.C.L.A. L. Rev. 647.

8. Rutherford v. United States, 399 F. Supp. 1208 (W.D. Okla. 1975); Carnohan v. United States, Civil Action No. 77–0010–GT, (S.D. Cal. Jan. 21, 1977); Rizzo v. United States, 432 F. Supp. 356 (E.D. N.Y. 1977).

9. Rutherford v. United States, 399 F. Supp. 1208 (W.D. Okla. 1975).

10. 442 U.S. 544 (1979).

11. 616 F.2d 455 (10th Cir. 1980).

12. CAL. HEALTH & SAFETY CODE, § 1707.1.

13. Suenram v. The Society of the Valley Hospital, 155 N.J. Super. 593 (1977).

14. 153 Cal. Rptr. 431 (1979).

14A. ARIZ. REV. STAT. ANN. § 32–1962 (Supp. 1977-78); DEL. CODE tit. 16, §§ 4901–4905 (Supp. 1977); FLA. STAT. ANN. §§ 395.066, 458.24, 459.24 (West Supp. 1979); ILL. ANN. STAT. ch. 56½, §§ 1801–1804, (Smith-Hurd Supp. 1978); IND. CODE ANN. §§ 16–8–8–1 to –6 (Burns 1977); LA. REV. STAT. ANN. § 40:676 (West 1977); NEV. REV. STAT. §§ 585.495, 630.303, 633.521, 639.2804, 639.2805 (1977); N.H. REV. STAT. ANN. § 329:30 (Supp. 1977); N.J. STAT. ANN. § 24:6F–1 to –5 (West Supp. 1978); OKLA. STAT. ANN. tit. 63, §§ 2–311.1 to .6 (West 1977); Ore. ch. 611, 1977; ORE. Laws 533; TEX. REV. CIV. STAT. ANN. art 4476–5a (Vernon Supp. 1978–79); WASH. REV. CODE ANN. § 70.54.130 to .150 (Supp. 1977).

15. See, e.g., ILL. ANN. STAT., ch. 56½, §§ 1801–1804.

16. See, e.g., FLA. STAT. ANN. §§ 395.066, 458.24 (West Cum. Supp. 1978); ORE. REV. STAT. § 689.885 (1977).

17. FLA. STAT. ANN. §§ 676, § 1285.1.

18. TEX. REV. CIV. STAT. ANN. art. 4476–5A.

19. TEX. REV. CIV. STAT. ANN. art. 4476–5A; LA. REV. STAT. ANN. § 676, § 1285.1.

20. ILL. ANN. STAT., ch. 56½, §§ 1801–1804.

21. FLA. STAT. ANN. §§ 395.066, 458.24 (West Cum. Supp. 1978); Pub. Act. 80–1096, 1977; Ill. Legis. Serv. 53 (West) (to be codified as ILL. ANN. STAT. ch. 56½, §§ 1801–1804 (Smith-Hurd)); IND. CODE ANN. §§ 16–8–8–1 to 16–8–8–7 (Burns Cum. Supp. 1978); LA. REV. STAT. ANN. § 1285.1 (West Cum. Supp. 1978), LA. REV. STAT. ANN. § 676 (West 1977); 1977 NEV. STATS. 1646 (to be codified as NEV. REV. STAT. §§ 585, 630, 633, 639); N.J. STAT. ANN. §§ 24:6F–1 to 24, 6F–5 (West

Cum. Supp. 1978–79); OKLA. STAT. ANN. tit. 63, §§ 2–313.1 to 2–313.6 (West Cum. Supp. 1978–79); WASH. REV. CODE. ANN. §§ 70.54.130 to 70.54.150 (Supp. 1977).

22. See, e.g., ILL. ANN. STAT., ch. 56½, §§ 1801–1804.

23. For a thorough judicial analysis of the toxicity of laetrile, see Custody of a Minor II, 378 Mass. 712, 393, N.E. 2d 836 (1979).

24. 21 U.S.C.A. § 812 (c) (a) (1976).

25. Shapiro, *The Right of Privacy and Heroin Use for Painkilling Purposes by the Terminally Ill Cancer Patient*, 21 Ariz. L. Rev. 41, 43–44 (1979).

26. R. Twycross, *Clinical Experience With Diamorphine in Advanced Malignant Disease*, 9 Intl. J. Clin. Pharma. Ther. Taxi., 184–98 (1974); R. Twycross and S. Wald, *Long Term Use of Diamorphine in Advanced Cancer*, 1 Advan. Pain Research Ther. 661 (1976); R. Twycross, *Choice of Strong Analgesic in Terminal Cancer: Diamorphine or Morphine?* 3 Pain 93 (1977).

26A. Kaiko et al, *Analgesic and Mood Effects of Heroin and Morphine in Cancer Patients with Postoperative Pain*, 304 N. Eng. J. Med. 1501 (June 18, 1981); Lasagna, *Heroin: A Medical "Me Too,"* 304 N. Eng. J. Med. 1539 (June 18, 1981).

27. H.R. 7334, 96th Congress, 1980; New York, Assembly Bill A. 12078 and Senate Bill S. 9098 (1978).

28. Shapiro, *The Right of Privacy and Heroin Use for Painkilling Purposes by the Terminally Ill Cancer Patient*, 21 Ariz. L. Rev. 41.

29. Sallan, Zinberg, and Frei, *Anti-Emetic Effective of Delta-9 Tetrahydracannabinol in Patients Receiving Chemotherapy for Cancer*, 293 N. Eng. J. Med. 795–97 (1975); Chang, et al, *Delta-9-THC as an Anti-Emetic in Cancer Patients Receiving High-Dose Methotrexate*, 91 Annals Intern. Med. 819–924 (1979); Hepler, *Pupillary Constriction After Marijuana Smoking*, 74 Amer. J. Opthal. 1185–90 (1972).

30. Controlled Substances Act, 21 U.S.C. § 812 (exc) (1976).

31. WASH. REV. CODE ANN. §69.51.040 (Supp. 1980); ORE. REV. STAT. §475.515 (1979); NEV. REV. STAT. §453.760 (1979); N.M. STAT. ANN. §26–24–4 (Supp. 1980); LA. REV. STAT. ANN. §1022 (West Supp. 1980); FLA. STAT. ANN. §402.36 (West Supp. 1980); IA.CODE ANN. §204.206 (West Supp. 1980); ILL. ANN. STAT. Ch. 56½, §711 (Smith Hurd Supp. 1980); W. VA. CODE §16–5A–7 (1979); VA. CODE §18.2–251.1 (Supp. 1980); ME. REV. STAT. §2404 (1980); TEX. REV. CIV. STAT. ANN. art. 4476–15 §7.01 (Vernon Supp. 1980); CAL. HEALTH & SAFETY CODE §11261 (West Supp. 1980); ALA. CODE tit. 20 §20–2–113 (Supp. 1980); ARIZ. REV. STAT. §36–1032 (Supp. 1980); COLO. REV. STAT. §25–5–904 (Supp. 1979); GA. CODE ANN. §84–904a (Supp. 1980); MICH. COMP. LAWS ANN. §333.7335 (Supp. 1980); OHIO REV. CODE ANN. §3719.85 (Page Supp. 1980); R.I. GEN. LAWS §28.4–1 (Supp. 1980); The Therapeutic Research Act, ch. 614, 1980 Minn. Sess. L. Service 1296 (to be codified as MINN. STAT. §152.21) (West 1980); Controlled Substances Therapeutic Research Act, ch. 810, 1980 Sess.

L. News of N.Y. 1323 (to be codified as N.Y. Public Health Law §3397) (McKinney 1980).

32. N.M. STAT. ANN. §26–2A–4 (Supp. 1980).
33. *Medical Necessity as a Defense to Criminal Liability: United States v. Randall,,* 46 Geo. Wash. L. Rev. 273 (1978).
34. United States v. Randall, 104 Daily Wash. L. Rep. 2240 (D.C. Super, Ct. Nov. 24, 1976).
35. Grinspoon and Bakalar, *Psychedelic Drugs Reconsidered* (1979).
36. E. Kluber-Ross, *On Death and Dying,* 112–38 (1969).
37. Controlled Substances Act, 21 U.S.C. §812 (c) (c), 1976.

III

The Right to Commit Suicide

Some critically ill persons find that their life is no longer worth living and wish to die. Refusing further medical care, however, may not lead to a quick, easy death. Such patients, particularly if chronically or terminally ill, may then decide to kill themsel·es, and may ask others for assistance in doing so. There is considerable public debate over the desirability of such practices. This chapter deals with the right of the critically ill patient to control the timing of his death through suicide.

Does a critically ill patient have a right to commit suicide?
Yes. Committing suicide (or self-murder or active euthanasia on oneself) was illegal at common law. However, criminal laws against attempted suicide have been repealed in nearly all states.[1] A critically ill person who sought to kill herself to speed up her death or gain relief from ·disability or chronic illness, would not be committing a crime. However, doctors, family, police, and others, could lawfully prevent such an attempt by physical interference, emergency treatment, or short-term psychiatric commitment.[2] The latter is unlikely with attempted suicide by critically ill persons, because their decision will usually be considered rational.

The chief legal consequence of a person killing herself will be the official recording of the death as a suicide, and in some cases, loss of life insurance benefits.

May a critically ill person sue a person who prevents him from committing suicide?
Probably not. Suits by a frustrated suicide are unlikely, and if they occurred, are unlikely to be successful. Emergency

room physicians are not liable for battery when they treat without consent, attempted suicides,[3] because there is uncertainty about the competency, or even the intent, of the patient. Similarly, a person would be privileged to physically restrain or prevent another person from committing suicide, even though such actions in other context, would be battery or false imprisonment. However, a situation could occur with a critically ill person where there was no question about the rationality, indeed, desirability of the suicide. Interference in that case could then be an actionable battery, for it would interfere with their liberty, and force additional suffering on them.

Does a competent consenting adult have the right to have another person kill him if he is unable to kill himself?
No. Actively killing another person, even with the patient's consent, is homicide even though well motivated. Although consensual homicide does not violate the deceased's rights, and the decision for death is a rational way to avoid terrible suffering, neither consent nor good intentions is an acceptable defense.

Cases of consensual homicide, or active euthanasia, are not uncommon and often are prosecuted. Depending on the facts of particular cases, juries may acquit or convict of less serious offenses. In the *Zygmaniak* case, for example, a twenty-six-year-old man who was paralyzed from the neck down from a motorcycle accident, asked his brother to kill him "to end his misery." The brother shot him in the intensive care unit. A jury in New Jersey acquitted him on grounds of temporary insanity.[4]

May a person assist or provide the means for a critically ill patient to take her own life?
No. Most states make it a crime to give another person a drug, poison, or weapon, with the intent or knowledge that the other person will use it to take her life, either by a specific statute on the subject, or as part of the law of homicide.[5] In the *Roberts* case,[6] for example, a bedridden victim of advanced multiple sclerosis asked her husband to place a cup of poison by her bed so that she might kill herself. He was prosecuted for murder after she took the poison and died on the ground that he had assisted a suicide.

It is unlikely, however, that a doctor who gave an elderly

patient sleeping pills, could be prosecuted merely because the patient later used the pills to kill himself. Without intent or knowledge that the pills would be used for this purpose, a person who happens to have provided another with the means for suicide, has not committed a crime.

As a practical matter, prosecutors and jurors may be reluctant to charge, and reluctant to convict or harshly penalize those who assist suicidal patients, particularly if the patient is terminal or chronically ill. Many proponents of a person's right to die think that helping those who cannot help themselves to die passively, should be lawful, even if active euthanasia is not.

May a critically ill person get books or manuals telling him how to commit suicide?

Yes. Several groups in England and the United States have, or are planning to publish, suicide manuals.[7] These books are important sources of information for critically ill persons who are contemplating suicide, but who are not familiar with painless, effective, accessible ways of doing so. The publication of such manuals might increase the number of suicides, both of those who have no other way to relieve their suffering, and those who are temporarily depressed or could have been reconciled to living.

While the publication, sale, or distribution of such manuals could be considered illegal, they could not be legally banned in the United States (though they have been in England).[8] The First Amendment protects all ideas, even those which might lead to undesirable activities, and thus would protect the publication and distribution of suicide manuals.[9] A person who gives another person a manual or instructions on committing suicide, with the intent or knowledge that a suicide will occur, would also have a First-Amendment defense. The state cannot prevent suicide by suppressing information on how to kill oneself.

NOTES

1. Schulman, *Suicide and Suicide Prevention: A Legal Analysis*, 54 Amer. Bar Assn. J. 855 (1968).
2. Greenberg, *Involuntary Psychiatric Commitments to Prevent Suicide*, 49 N.Y.U. L. Rev. 227 (1974).

3. Chayet, Legal Implications of Emergency Case 45 (1969).
4. Veatch, *Death, Dying and the Biological Revolution*, 79, 82 (1976).
5. LaFave and Scott, Criminal Law, 570–71 (1972).
6. People v. Roberts, 211 Mich. 187, 178 N.W. 690 (1920).
7. "Right-to-Die Groups Seek Another Right: To Aid in Suicide," *Wall Street Journal*, Sept. 4, 1980, p. 1.
8. "Publication of Suicide Guide Reviews a Debate in Britain," *New York Times*, Sept. 28, 1980, p. 20A.
9. Brandenburg v. Ohio, 395 U.S. 444, 447 (1969). J. Nowak, R. Rotunda, and J. Young, Constitutional Law 790-94 (1978).

IV

The Right to Refuse Treatment

The situation of critical illness most often dealt with by the courts, concerns competent adults who refuse medical treatment necessary to keep them alive. Until recently, most of these cases involved religious objectors such as Jehovah's Witnesses or Christian Scientists. With the development of life-prolonging medical technology, such groups as the elderly, the terminally ill, and the severely disabled, also wish to avoid the burdens of medical treatment.

Typically, the patient refuses a medical procedure that could prolong his life. He may object because of the nature of the medical intervention, or the life-situation in which successful treatment will leave him. His family or doctors or officials of the state, disagree with the choice and think the patient should live. They may find his choice to be misguided, irrational, uninformed, or even immoral. In some cases they may try to have him treated against his will.

The courts are now drawing upon the Anglo-American tradition of individual autonomy and self-determination, and constitutional rights of privacy, to resolve these conflicts. This chapter discusses the right of a competent adult patient to refuse treatment.

May a competent adult refuse medical care necessary to keep him alive?

In general, yes. The right of self-determination and autonomy central to American law is now recognized, and includes the right of a competent adult to reject life-saving medical care. This right is an application of the rule of informed consent to medical treatment. Under this rule, no doctor may treat a competent patient without his free, know-ing consent. While the United States Supreme Court has not yet addressed the question, influential state courts have found the right to reject life-saving medical care to be part of the fundamental constitutional right of privacy.[1] As a constitu-tional right, the state must show very strong reasons for intervening with an individual's exercise of the right.

May a terminally ill person refuse medical treatment that would keep her alive?

Yes. If the patient is terminally ill, her right to refuse treatment will be recognized. The courts would find no com-pelling state interest served by prolonging the dying process of such a person.

The reasoning behind this position is clearly seen in a Massachusetts case that upheld the right of an incurable cancer patient to decline care when "the disease clearly indi-cates that life will soon, and inevitably be extinguished."[2] The court stated:

> The interest of the State in prolonging a life must be reconciled with the interest of an individual to reject the traumatic cost of that prolongation. There is a substantial distinction in the State's insistence that human life be saved where the affliction is curable, as opposed to the State interest, where, as here, the issue is not whether but when, for how long, and at what cost to the individ-ual that life may be briefly extended. . . . The constitu-tional right to privacy . . . is an expression of the sanctity of individual choice and self-determination as fundamen-tal constituents of life. The value of life as so perceived is lessened not by a decision to refuse treatment, but by the failure to allow a competent human being the right of choice.[3]

The New Jersey Supreme Court adopted a similar position in the famous *Quinlan* case when it discussed the right of an irreversibly comatose patient to refuse treatment. It stated that while the courts might require treatment in a situation where the patient is "salvable to long life and vibrant health," they would not intervene where the patient is "terminally ill, riddled by cancer and suffering great pain," or is irreversibly doomed "to vegetate a few measurable months with no realistic possibility of returning to any semblance of cognitive or sapient life."[4] In the court's view

> the state's interest [in preserving life] . . . weakens and the individual's right to privacy grows as the degree of bodily invasion increases and the prognosis dims. Ultimately there comes a point at which the individual's right overcomes State interest.[5]

The right of a terminally ill person to refuse necessary medical care is also well illustrated in the *Perlmutter* case.[6] Joseph Perlmutter, a seventy-three-year-old former taxi driver and athlete, came down with amyotrophic lateral sclerosis (Lou Gerhig's disease), a degenerative terminal disease that left him respirator dependent. He did not wish to continue to live in this state, and pulled out the breathing tube, but the doctors, out of fear of legal liability, reinserted it. A lawyer brought his case to court. The judge ruled that his constitutional right of privacy and self-determination gave him the right to stay off the respirator, even if it meant that he would die, and ordered the doctors to stop the respirator.

May a competent patient who is not terminally ill, refuse necessary medical treatment?

Yes. The right to refuse medical treatment is a right held by all competent adults, not just those who are terminally ill. However, like all rights, it is not absolute and can be restricted to serve important or compelling state interests, such as preserving life, protecting minors, protecting innocent third parties, preventing suicide, and maintaining the ethical integrity of the medical profession. (The right of prison inmates to refuse necessary medical treatment may be more limited because of the effect of such refusals on prison discipline).[6A]

When the person is not terminally ill, doctors will be more reluctant to honor the patient's refusal, and courts are more likely to find the state's interests compelling. If the medical treatment necessary to keep the patient alive is not highly intrusive or painful, and the patient will be restored to a healthful condition, the courts are more likely to find that these interests outweigh the patient's interest in self-determination.

For example, the state's interest in preserving life may

justify overriding the patient's refusal, because there would be no burden on the patient beyond the failure to follow his wishes. Thus, courts in Jehovah's Witness cases will generally order blood transfusions as long as the patient does not believe he will be damned forever if he receives it.[7] The court order violates the patient's choice, but does not impose any other suffering on the patient.

On the other hand, if intrusive, painful, or prolonged medical procedures are necessary, or the patient will end up in a severely disabled or debilitated state, it is unlikely that courts would order treatment. Such cases could arise with severely burned patients, paraplegics or quadraplegics, persons facing amputation for gangrene, cancer patients in need of radiation and chemotherapy, or Jehovah's Witnesses who believe that blood transfusions will damn them forever. Forcing treatment in such situations would lessen the value of life rather than preserve it, and the courts are unlikely to order it.

Several cases illustrating this point have arisen with patients who refuse amputation. The *Quackenbush*[8] case is typical. A seventy-two-year-old man living alone in a trailer, was brought to the hospital emergency room and found to be suffering from severe gangrene caused by advanced arterio-sclerosis. The doctors predicted that unless both legs were amputated, he would die within three weeks. When he refused, the hospital asked the courts to find him incompetent and to appoint a guardian to consent to the life-saving surgery. The court found that he was competent and had the right to refuse the amputation, despite the fact that he was not terminally ill and could live indefinitely if the operation were done. The state's interest in the preservation of life was not sufficient to outweigh his right of privacy. The operation would be highly invasive—amputation of both legs above the knee and possibly the thigh. He would probably be confined to a wheelchair for the rest of his life and be forced to move to a nursing home. The court upheld his refusal; forcing a person who is ready to accept death to undergo major surgery and amputation, and live as an invalid in a nursing home, would lessen, rather than enhance, the value of life, and thus not constitute a compelling state interest.

May a competent adult with children refuse necessary medical treatment?

Yes and no. The courts frequently cite protection of children as a reason for overriding a competent patient's refusal of treatment, a situation most likely to arise with Jehovah's Witness parents who refuse blood transfusions. But no court has ever ordered a clearly competent patient to be treated against her wishes, solely to protect minor children. In the famous *Georgetown Hospital* case[9] often cited as an authority for this position, a blood transfusion was ordered for a twenty-three-year-old mother of a three-year-old injured in an auto-mobile accident, despite her apparent religious objections. However, the transfusion probably would have been ordered even if there were no child, since the patient was incompe-tent at the time; it was an emergency; and her true wishes, including her beliefs about compelled transfusions, could not be ascertained. In another case, a blood transfusion was or-dered for a Jehovah's Witness woman in order to protect the fetus; she was eight months pregnant.[10] However, this case arose before *Roe* v. *Wade*[11] gave the mother the right to terminate a pregnancy for any reason, in the first six months.

In other cases, the courts have refused to order treatment over the objections of a parent of minor children. In the *Osborne* case,[12] a thirty-four-year-old Jehovah's Witness with two young children, needed blood transfusions to save his life after a tree fell on him. He refused treatment, and his wife agreed. The court upheld his refusal, despite the grief it might cause the children.

The exact extent to which the existence of minor children will override the parents' refusal thus remains unclear. The courts will be most inclined to override the patient's choice when children are involved. But a close scrutiny of the competing interests will often show that the harmful effects of forcing treatment on the patient, is greater than the burdens on a child whose parent dies by a conscientious refusal of medical treatment.

The strongest case for ordering treatment for the sake of children, would be where the child's life depended on it, as is shown by a decision of the Georgia Supreme Court in *Jeffer-son* v. *Griffin-Spaulding County Hospital Authority*.[12A] A woman who was thirty-nine weeks pregnant had placenta previa, a condition which, unless a Caesarean section were done, was very likely to cause a stillbirth and the mother's death as well. The mother refused. A court hearing was held to protect the interests of the unborn child and resulted in the decision that the Caesarean section be done. Where the child's life is not directly threatened, the case for imposing medical treatment against a person's wishes is much weaker.

May the spouse or other family members who disagree with the competent patient's refusal of treatment, force treatment against his will?

No. The family does not have the right to control the health care given a competent adult—only the adult himself has this right. The right of autonomy and self-determination in health care is a right against interference by the family, as well as by doctors and the state. Doctors who treated at the family's behest would be violating the patient's rights and could be sued. They should never do so without first obtaining court approval for overriding the patient's refusal, which is unlikely to be granted unless the patient has minor children or other factors justifying a limitation on the right to refuse treatment exist.

What if the doctors disagree with the patient's choice to refuse medical care?

Doctors have sometimes asserted a right to save a life by treating an unwilling patient in order to fulfill professional or ethical obligations. Courts often recognize this concern.[13] It was a significant factor in the *Heston* case[14] which involved a twenty-two-year-old unmarried woman who ruptured her spleen in an automobile accident and needed a blood transfusion. She was a Jehovah's Witness, and appeared incompetent at the time, even though her mother insisted that she would not accept blood and refused to consent on her behalf. The judge called at 1:30 A.M. to hear the question appointed a guardian to consent to the transfusion. The operation was performed and the woman survived. She then sought to vacate the order, but the judge's order was upheld by the New Jersey Supreme Court, which relied, in part, on the medical profession's standards:

When the hospital and staff are thus involuntary hosts and their interests are pitted against the belief of the patient, we think it reasonable to resolve the problem by permitting the hospital and its staff to pursue their functions according to their professional standards.[15]

While such concerns are likely to be recognized in emergency situations where the patient's competency and wishes may not be clearly established, in nonemergencies, the doctor's interest in preserving life ordinarily will not outweigh the patient's interest. A Massachusetts case, for example, recognized that the right to bodily integrity and self-determination contained in doctrines of informed consent and privacy, are "superior to the institutional considerations" of hospitals and the medical profession.[16] Otherwise, doctors could always ignore patient wishes and thus eliminate self-determination in medical care.

Has the person who dies because he has rejected medical care committed suicide?

Probably not, though the courts have not directly faced the question. Suicide means the intentional termination of one's life. Usually this occurs by active means, but the concept is broad enough to include such suicidal methods as starving oneself, or refusing medical care.[17]

For legal purposes, the question of whether a death caused by the refusal of necessary medical care is a suicide, may depend upon the legal context, or reason for asking the question. Classifying a death as suicide could affect (a) the cause of death listed on the death certificate, (b) the life insurance benefits, (c) the criminal liability of persons who assist the patient in avoiding medical care, and (d) the patient's right to refuse medical treatment.

Death Certificate

The death certificate is completed by the doctor who determines that death has occurred. While there is no uniform practice among doctors, it is likely that persons who die from refusing care, would not be considered suicides. A doctor's statement that such a death is from natural causes, is not likely to be challenged by a coroner, who has the power to hold inquests and determine the cause of death.

Life Insurance

Most states now require that life insurance benefits be paid for deaths by suicide, usually after the policy has been in effect for a minimum period, such as two years, although this wasn't so in the past.[18] Where the exclusion of suicide is applicable, the question of benefits for death from refusal of medical care, has not yet been decided by the courts. It is unlikely that the courts would consider death from the refusal of treatment as suicide, where the patient was terminally ill, or wanted to live but could not accept certain treatments, such as blood transfusions. Indeed, states with living will laws usually provide that withholding care in accordance with the patient's directive, does not constitute suicide, or affect life insurance benefits.[19]

Assisting Suicidal Patients

People who remove respirators or feeding tubes, would probably not be criminally liable. In the *Perlmutter* case (see p. 34) the Florida court held that the removal of a seventy-three-year-old man with Lou Gerhig's disease from a respirator essential to keep him alive, was not self-murder, and that people who assist him could not be prosecuted for assisting a suicide.[20]

Right to Refuse Treatment

Whether refusal is suicide is also important, because some courts have stated that the state's interest in preventing suicide may override the patient's refusal of treatment. However, if the patient is terminally ill or severely disabled, the refusal of treatment would probably not be considered suicide because the state's interest

. . . lies in the prevention of irrational self-destruction. What we consider here is a competent, rational decision to refuse treatment when death is inevitable and the treatment offers no hope of cure or preservation of life. There is no connection between the conduct here in issue and any State concern to prevent suicide.[21]

If the patient is not terminally ill, courts may distinguish the patient's refusal from suicide on the ground that the patient did not set the death producing agent in motion, or does not have a specific intent to die, but for religious or other reasons cannot accept medical treatment.[22] If the patient's decision seems truly irrational and not understandable within his own religious or philosophical belief system, the courts could treat it as a suicide attempt and override the patient's refusal, or more likely find the patient to be incompetent with no right to refuse treatment.

When is a patient competent to refuse medical care?

A patient is competent if she can understand the nature of a proposed treatment and the consequences if it is not given, and is capable of exercising choice. The patient need not understand the medical theory behind a course of treatment, as long as she understands the nature and consequences of the choice. Also, she can be competent to make decisions about medical care without also being competent to manage her property, make a will, or do other legal acts.

Competency may also be independent of whether or not a person is mentally ill. Thus, persons committed to mental institutions have been found competent to decide about their medical care, because their mental illness was not found to interfere with their ability to understand the nature and consequences of proposed treatment.[22A] In the *Yetter*[23] case, a woman in a mental institution was considered competent enough to refuse a biopsy for suspected breast cancer because the court was convinced that she understood the nature of the procedure and the consequences of refusing. She later died of breast cancer.

The meaning of competency—and the difficulties the determination sometimes involves—may be illustrated by two cases involving elderly women who refused the amputation of their gangrenous feet that had developed due to advancing arteriosclerosis. In *Lane* v. *Candura*[24] a lower court had granted a petition appointing the daughter of a diabetic seventy-seven-year-old widow to be her mother's guardian for purposes of consenting to this operation. This decision was reversed and Mrs. Candura's right to refuse the amputation was upheld because the appeals court found ample evidence that she was aware of the consequences of refusing the operation, even though her sense of time was distorted; her train of thought sometimes wandered or was confused; and she often was defensive or combative in responses to questions. She did not want the operation because she has been unhappy since the death of her husband; she does not wish to be a burden on her children; she does not believe that the operation will cure her; she does not wish to live as an invalid or in a nursing home; and she does not fear death but welcomes it.[25]

Though her refusal seemed irrational to her doctors, it did not mean she was incompetent in the legal sense, for her forgetfulness and confusion did not impair "her ability to understand that in rejecting the amputation, she is, in fact, choosing death over life."[26]

In the Matter of Northern,[27] by contrast, an appeals court upheld a finding that a seventy-two-year-old woman was incompetent to refuse the amputation of her gangrenous feet because of evidence suggesting that she did not fully appreciate the consequences of the decision. Though she was generally lucid and of sound mind,

> on the subjects of death and amputation of her feet her comprehension is blocked, blinded or dimmed to the extent that she is incapable of recognizing facts which would be obvious to a person of normal perception.
>
> For example, in the presence of this Court, the patient looked at her feet and refused to recognize the obvious fact that the flesh was dead, black, shriveled, rotting and stinking.
>
> The record also discloses that the patient refuses to consider the eventuality of death which is or ought to be obvious in the face of such dire bodily deterioration.[28]

While this case may be criticized for not allowing persons who deny the existence of their medical situation to be found competent,[29] it shows that persons who do understand the alternatives, will be found competent.

Must a competent patient's refusal of treatment be followed if he later becomes incompetent?

Probably, though courts have not squarely answered the question. The implication of *Lane v. Candura, Quackenbush,* and other cases that have found persons to be competent to decide against necessary treatment, is that their choices are to be followed, even if they later become so confused and disoriented that they no longer can understand the nature and consequences of the treatment they are rejecting. Similarly, courts have upheld, though not invariably, the right of adult Jehovah's Witnesses not to have blood transfusions administered even if they are incompetent to decide at the time that the blood is needed, as long as their objections were clearly made while competent.[30] This principle was recognized by a trial judge in a New York case when a 41-year-old diabetic who had become blind and had both legs amputated wanted to stop the dialysis treatment keeping him alive. He was found competent by two psychiatrists, but the hospital sought a judicial order to keep treating him. Before a court hearing could be held, he lapsed into a coma. The court eventually upheld the refusal of treatment, even though the patient was now incompetent, because he had been competent when he refused treatment.[30A]

There are two reasons why the courts are likely to follow the competent person's wishes against medical care when they become incompetent. One is a policy interest in allowing competent persons to control medical interactions that occur when one becomes incompetent (see Chapter VIII, Advanced Directives and Living Wills). The second is that treatment and the prolonged life that it provides, will not be in the interests of the person who becomes incompetent anymore than when he was competent. Mrs. Candura and Mr. Quackenbush wished to avoid suffering by refusing amputation; their decision would be upheld if they became incompetent. However, there may be situations in which an incompetent person, if now able to communicate his preferences, would no longer wish his prior refusal of treatment to be honored. In ascertaining an incompetent person's choice, this possibility has to be kept in mind. The mere fact of incompetency, however, does not mean that choices expressed while competent can be ignored.

Can a patient be considered competent if she has intermittent periods of lucidity or is under medication?

Yes, though it will depend on the facts of each case. Senility, medication, diabetes, liver problems, and other conditions in which the patient has intermittent periods of lucidity, might make it very difficult to tell whether the patient is competent to refuse treatment. Choices made in a period of lucidity should be honored, even if he had earlier been, or later becomes, incompetent.

An interesting example of how a person can be found competent to reject necessary treatment despite earlier periods of incompetency, occurred in the *Quackenbush* case (see p. 35). The hospital believed that the seventy-two-year-old man who refused amputation of his gangrenous legs was incompetent and asked the courts to appoint a guardian to consent to the operation. At the hearing, a psychiatrist testified that the patient was disoriented as to time and place and not aware that he was in a hospital or talking to a doctor or nurse, and was suffering from visual hallucinations. He diagnosed the condition as an organic brain syndrome and stated that the patient was not competent to make an informed decision about the operation. Another psychiatrist who examined the patient five days later, found that the patient had no hallucinations, understood that he had gangrene and could die without the amputation, and thus was competent. The judge talked with the patient one day later and also found him competent to make an informed choice about the operation:

> He did not hallucinate, his answers to my questions were responsive and he seemed reasonably alert. His conversation did wander occasionally but to no greater extent than would be expected of a seventy-two-year-old man in his circumstances. He spoke somewhat philosophically about his circumstances and desires. He hopes for a miracle but realizes there is no great likelihood of its occurrence. He indicates a desire . . . to return to his trailer and live out his life. He is not experiencing any pain and indicates that if he does, he could change his mind about having the operation.[31]

Who determines competency?

Legally a person is presumed to be competent unless declared otherwise by a court. As a practical matter, the doctor treating the patient will determine first of all, whether there are such doubts about a person's competency that the patient's decisions for medical care need not be followed. He may consult nurses, family members, and the patient, or call in other doctors or psychiatrists. If he believes that the patient is incompetent, he should ask the courts to have the patient declared incompetent and a guardian appointed to consent to medical care.

In many cases, however, doctors may simply decide that

the patient is incompetent and get the consent of the next of kin. There may often be no legal consequences from handling the matter in this way, particularly if the patient is benefited and the kin could have been appointed guardian. However, doctors who make such decisions on their own, may erroneously conclude that a patient is incompetent and thus deny the patient the right to make his own choice. To avoid such errors and possible suits for damages, they should seek an official determination of competency and, if necessary, the appointment of a guardian.

Can a patient be found incompetent merely because he refuses medical care that the doctors want to give?

Not legally. Doctors will generally not question the competency of patients who consent to treatments that the doctor recommends. However, when the patient refuses the doctor may suspect his mental competency and seek to have a guardian appointed in order to be able to treat him. This is more likely to occur when the doctor's personal beliefs are different than the patient's, and the doctor is not able to separate out his moral and personal views from his medical judgment. In *Lane* v. *Candura*, (see p. 40), the doctors regarded Mrs. Candura as competent to consent to medical care until she changed her mind and withdrew consent to the amputation. In their view she was making an irrational choice because she gave life a lower priority than they would. But the refusal of medical care alone—despite the feeling of many doctors—is not proof that a person does not understand the nature and consequences of a proposed treatment and thus is incompetent. To protect their right to refuse care, patients should explain to the doctor their reasons for refusal and that they fully understand the choice. They should also inform their family or friends who might aid them if doctors seek to have them declared incompetent when they refuse or disagree about the care offered.

What should families and doctors who are uncertain about the patient's competency do when he refuses treatment?

Since a competent adult patient, particularly one who is terminally ill, has a right to decline necessary medical care, doctors and families are obligated to honor this wish. (A court could order them to pay damages or stop treatment if this is done without the patient's consent.) On the other hand, doctors would have a legal duty to treat incompetent patients as long as treatment is in their interests. Doctors could be liable for manslaughter or wrongful death if they negligently conclude that a patient is competent and accept his refusal of treatment.

If there are doubts about a person's competency, the doctors should obtain psychiatric consultation. If the consultant advises that the patient is competent, the doctor may legally honor his refusal of treatment (indeed, would be obligated to). To be certain, however, as might be desirable if the patient's refusal of care could lead to death, the doctor might request a judicial determination of competency. In such a proceeding a guardian *ad litem* and attorney should be appointed to represent the patient.

If consultations suggest that the patient is incompetent, a guardian should be appointed to make decisions about medical care. A judicial decision will give the parties some certainty about the legality of their actions, and may prevent the abuse of a patient who is helpless to protect his right to have care withheld.

What can happen to a doctor who treats a competent patient against his will, in order to keep him alive?

Doctors sometimes treat competent patients against their will because they believe the patient's decision is unwise or morally wrong, because the family wants treatment, or because the doctor fears legal liability if she fails to do everything possible to save the patient.

Such a doctor can be sued for damages for battery, false imprisonment, or lack of informed consent, and may be responsible for the cost of medical care. The patient or his family would need legal services to bring the suit, and would have to prove that the doctor knew, or should have known, that the patient was competent to refuse care. Such suits have been rare, and might not result in large damage awards, if the patient were claiming a right to die.

There have also been suits to protect the right of the patient not to be treated over his wishes, or to prevent unwanted treatment in the future. For example, Jehovah's Witnesses who have been treated against their will have gone to court to enjoin such interventions in the future, or to have court orders for blood transfusions vacated.[32]

A patient with a lawyer or family or friends to help him,

can also go to court to order the doctor to stop treatment. In the *Perlmutter* case (see p. 34), when the doctors refused to allow the patient to turn off his respirator himself, he got a court to rule that he had a right to determine his own care and to order the doctors to allow him to leave the hospital. A doctor who then refused would be in contempt of court.

Can a competent patient exercise her right to refuse treatment before the need for treatment arises?

Yes. It is clear in states with living will laws, and probably in states without them, that a competent patient can arrange that necessary care—respirators, drugs, surgery, and so forth—be withheld at some future time when the patient is no longer competent to decide. In some states doctors and families can be obligated to withhold treatment on this basis. In other states, directives made while competent, may protect doctors who follow them from liability for withholding care, but do not obligate doctors to do so. The extent of this right is discussed in chapter VIII.

In several cases, courts have given effect to the prior expressed wishes of Jehovah's Witnesses who reject blood transfusions, even if the patient is presently incompetent, though this has not always been the case.[33] In another case, a Christian Scientist whose beliefs against medical care were well-known, could not be forced to receive psychotropic medication in a mental institution when she became mentally ill and incompetent.[34] The reasoning of these cases is likely to be extended to other decisions to reject medical care made while the patient is competent and to take effect when the patient becomes incompetent.

Does a competent patient have a right to die at home?

Yes. If a competent person is critically ill, he has a right to refuse further care, including hospital care, and cannot be put in a hospital against his will. No law requires that a person die in a hospital or under a doctor's care, or prohibits dying at home.

Although eighty percent of deaths now occur in hospitals,[35] there is a growing recognition that death may be more easily accepted when it occurs in the supportive setting of one's home. The hospice movement has facilitated dying at home, and the number of people choosing this option is likely to increase. As a practical matter, however, if family members object, they may be able to prevent a critically ill person from carrying out a desire to die at home. Disputes with family members on this question are not likely to reach the courts.

NOTES

1. Matter of Quinlan, 70 N.J. 10, 355 A.2d 647 (1975); Superintendent of Belchertown v. Saikewicz, 373 Mass. 728, 370 N.E. 2d 417 (1977); Satz v. Perlmutter, 63 So. 2d 160 Fla. App. 1978, 363 So. 2d 160 (1978); Eichner v. Dillon, 426 N.Y.S. 2d 157 (1980).
2. Superintendent of Belchertown v. Saikewicz, 373 Mass. 728, 370 N.E. 2d 417 (1977).
3. *Id.*
4. Matter of Quinlan, 70 N.J. 10, 355 A.2d 647 (1975).
5. *Id.*
6. Satz v. Perlmutter, 63 So. 2d 160 Fla. App. 1978, 363 So. 2d 160 (1978).
6A. Commissioner of Corrections v. Myers, 399 N.E. 2d 452, (Mass. 1979). State ex rel. White v. Narick, 292 S.E. 2d 54 (W. Va. 1982). The Georgia Supreme Court, however, has recognized the prisoner's right to refuse. Zant v. Prevatte, 286 S.E. 2d 715 (Ga. 1982).
7. United States v. George, 239 F. Supp. 752 (1965); Powell v. Columbian Presbyterian Medical Center, 49 Misc. 2d 215, 267 N.Y.S. 2d 450 (1965).
8. *In re* Quackenbush, 156 N.J. Super. 282, 383 A.2d 785 (1978).
9. Application of President and Directors of Georgetown College, 331 F.2d 1000 (D.C. Cir.), *cert. denied,* 377 U.S. 978 (1964).
10. Raleigh Fitkin—Paul Morgan Memorial Hospital v. Anderson, 42 N.J. 421, 201 A.2d 537 (1964), *cert. denied,* 377 U.S. 985.
11. Roe v. Wade, 410 U.S. 113 (1973).
12. *In re* Osborne, 294 A.2d 372 (D.C. 1972).
12A. 247 Ga. 8b 274 S.E. 2d 457 (1981). A Colorado court has also ordered that a Caesarean section be done over a mother's wishes. This case is reported in Bowes, W. A. and B. Selgestad, *Fetal versus Maternal Right: Medical and Legal Perspectives,* 58 Amer. J. Obstet. Gynecol. 209–14 (1981).
13. Application of President and Director of Georgetown College, 311 F.2d 1000 (D.C. Cir.), *cert. denied,* 377 U.S. 978 (1964).
14. John F. Kennedy Memorial Hospital V. Heston, 58 N.J. 576, 279 A.2d 670 (1971).
15. *Id.*
16. Superintendent of Belchertown v. Saikewicz, 373 Mass. 738, 370 N.E. 2d 417 (1977).

17. Beauchamp, "Suicide," in *Matters of Life and Death*, ed. Tom Regan, 67 (1980).

18. N.Y. Ins. Law §155 (2) (d) (McKinney 1966).

19. CAL. HEALTH & SAFETY CODE § 7192(a) (West Supp. 1980).

20. Satz v. Perlmutter, Fla. App., 363 So. 2d 160 (1978).

21. Superintendent of Belchertown v. Saikewicz, 373 Mass. 728, 370 N.E. 2d 417 (1977).

22. Buchanan, Medical Paternalism or Legal Imperialism, 5 Am. J. Law & Med. 97 (1979).

22A. This right has been recognized even when the medical care is directed at treating the mental illness that is the cause of their commitment. See New York City Health and Hospitals Corporation v. Stein, 335 N.Y.S. 2d 461 (1972); Rogers v. Okin, 478 F. Supp. 1342 (D. Mass. 1979).

23. *In re* Maida Yetter, 62 Pa. D&C 2d 619 (1973).

24. Lane v. Candura, 1978 Mass. Adv. Sh. 588, 376 N.E. 2d 1232 (Mass. App. 1978).

25. *Id*.

26. *Id*.

27. Department of Human Services v. Northern, 563 S.W. 2d 197 (Tenn. Ct. of Appeals, 1978).

28. *Id*.

29. Culver, Ferrell, and Green, *"ECT and Special Problems of Informed Consent,"* 137 Amer. J. Psych. 5, 1980.

30. *In re* Brooks, 32 Ill. 2d 361, 205 N.E. 2d 435 (1965).

30A. "Diabetic Dies After L.I. Judge Stops His Life Sustaining Care," *New York Times*, Oct. 23, 1982, p. 1, col. 4.

31. *In re* Quackenbush, 156 N.J. Super. 282, 383 A.2d 785 (1978).

32. John F. Kennedy Memorial Hospital v. Heston, 58 N.J. 576, 279 A.2d 670 (1971); Holmes v. Silver Cross Memorial Hospital, 340 F. Supp. 125 (N.D. Ill. 1972); Jehovah's Witnesses in the State of Washington v. King County Hospital, 278 F. Supp. 488 (1967).

33. John F. Kennedy Memorial Hospital v. Heston, 58 N.J. 576, 279 A.2d 670 (1971).

34. Winters v. Miller, 446 F.2d 65 (2nd Cir. 1971); *In re* Lucille Boyd, 403 A.2d 744 (1979).

35. G. Annas, The Rights of Hospital Patients, 162 (1975).

V

The Right to Stop Treatment on Incompetent Patients

Some of the hardest questions in the care of the critically ill arises with patients who are not competent to make choices about their treatment. Patients may lack the capacity to consent because of mental retardation, mental illness, senility, brain damage, or major organ failure. Their incompetency may be irreversible or temporary. They may also be terminally ill or in no danger of dying if properly treated. Finally, incompetent persons differ in their level of awareness. Some are comatose, while others are conscious and interact with others.

Since such patients cannot consent, there is no ready benchmark for knowing when treatment can be stopped. Vigorous treatment and prolonged life is not in the interest of all incompetent patients. When it is burdensome and has no compensating benefit, it can, and should, be withheld. At the same time, vigorous treatment that prolongs life with minimal suffering, should be provided if incompetent patients are to be shown equal respect.

In practice, doctors and families have had considerable discretion in deciding when treatment on such patients is to be terminated. But their decision may be motivated by competing interests, or by incomplete information; they also may be moved by the intense stress of critical illness. Since incompetent patients are entirely dependent and vulnerable, there is a danger that the needs of others will control, rather than those of the patient's.

Since the courts are just now grappling with the task of defining the rules that apply to the continuation of treatment on incompetent persons, the law here is particularly uncer-

49

tain. Most states have not yet enacted laws or decided cases in this area. The few cases that have been decided—in New York, New Jersey, and Massachusetts—are thus very influential and are likely to be followed by other states. Yet these cases have answered only a few of the many legal questions that arise. This chapter discusses the law that is now developing.

Does a critically ill incompetent patient have a right to be treated?

Yes. As long as the treatment will benefit the patient by relieving discomfort or by extending his life for a significant period of time and is not excessively burdensome, he has a right to be treated. The mentally impaired have the same right to treatment as the mentally normal. A person does not lose the right to necessary medical care just because she is retarded, mentally ill, senile, comatose, terminally ill, or otherwise incompetent, even though some patients in each of those categories may at some point have treatment legally stopped.

Doctors who have undertaken to care for a patient who is, or has become, incompetent, have a duty to treat the patient as long as treatment is beneficial. An intentional or negligent failure to provide proper treatment would constitute abandonment of the patient, and as with competent patients, could lead to civil liability, criminal sanctions, or disciplinary proceedings against the doctor.

When does an incompetent patient's right to treatment end?

It depends. Treatment may be stopped when it will no longer benefit the patient, either because it does not provide a longer or better quality of life, or because its burdens seem excessive. It is often said that such treatments can be withheld because they are "extraordinary" or "heroic." Since these terms incorporate a conclusion about whether the benefits of treatment to the patient are justified by its burdens and do not directly tell us which medical treatments are required, it is better to address directly, the question of benefits and burdens.

In assessing benefits to the patient, the pain and suffering of the treatment itself, as well as the resulting state or quality of life, will be considered. Thus, a treatment that would prolong a very impaired life and be itself very painful, would probably not be required. On the other hand, treatments that keep patients alive without undue suffering, but do not relieve incompetency, cannot be withheld, just because the patient is mentally retarded or senile.

The law's basic approach to treatment decisions for incompetents is a patient-centered one that gives primary regard to the needs and interests of the incompetent patient, rather than the needs and interests of families, doctors, and society, with whom the patient's interests may conflict.[1] The patient's diminished ability, mental status, or social worth, are not valid grounds for ignoring his interests. Equal respect for persons requires that incompetent patients not be denied treatment to serve the interests of others.

The courts, however, have not yet agreed on the test or standard for determining the patient's interests. Massachusetts and New Jersey, the states with the most experience in this area, have adopted the substituted judgment test for determining what should be done for an incompetent patient.[2] This test attempts to treat the incompetent patient as a choosing individual, by asking what he would choose if cognizant of his interests and able to communicate his choices. But unless the patient when competent had expressed a preference on the subject, it is difficult to infer any choice for an incompetent patient other than that which would protect his current best interests, viewed in his particular circumstances as a critically ill incompetent patient.

A less confusing approach, when there is no prior expression of preference, to the substituted judgment procedure of asking what the patient would choose if competent, is to ask directly whether treatment, in light of the additional life it makes possible and the burdens it entails, serves the patient's interest. Indeed, when properly understood, the best interests and substituted judgment tests should reach identical results, for an incompetent patient, if competent and able to make rational choices, would choose what would best serve his interests.[3]

The situations in which an incompetent person's right to treatment ends, will thus depend on whether or not, under the substituted judgment or a best interests test, he would find medical treatment to be in his interest. This will depend on the facts of each case—diagnosis, prognosis, treatment alternatives, therapeutic discomforts, and the prospect of recovery—rather than on the type of treatment proposed. In some cases, an incompetent patient might have a right to have respirator care, while in others, he has a right to have it discontinued. In any event, the courts are likely to respect the judgments of physicians and families who stop treatment on the basis of good faith assessments of what an incompetent patient would choose or what would best save his interests. The following questions discuss more specifically, situations in which treatment may no longer serve the interests of an incompetent patient, and therefore may be stopped.

May treatment be stopped on an incompetent patient who is irreversibly comatose?

Yes. The *Quinlan* case,[4] which is likely to be followed by other courts, held that patients who are irreversibly comatose, or in a persistent vegetative state, are deemed to have no further interest in living, and therefore can have necessary medical care stopped.

In *Quinlan*, a twenty-two-year-old unmarried woman suffered irreversible brain damage and became comatose. Because some brain function remained, she was still legally alive, and with treatment, could live indefinitely. The doctors described her as being in a "chronic persistent vegetative state," with no cognitive or sapient functioning, and no possibility of recovery.

After several months in a comatose condition, Ms. Quinlan's parents asked the doctors to discontinue the respirator. The doctors refused, claiming that it was their professional duty to maintain the patient's life as long as possible. Ms. Quinlan's father then asked a court to appoint him her guardian so that he would have legal authority to refuse further care. The trial court refused this petition, and he appealed to the New Jersey Supreme Court, which in a landmark decision, held that necessary medical care could be withheld from a chronically vegetative patient.

The court concluded that if Ms. Quinlan were competent, she would have a right to stop the respirator, because the state's interest in preserving life would be insufficient to overcome the patient's interest in avoiding a prolonged existence in such a debilitated condition. It then held that the competent patient's right to decline care "should not be discarded solely on the basis that her condition prevents her conscious exercise of the choice."[5] Instead, the privacy right of incompetent persons could be protected by permitting "the guardian and family . . . to render their best judgment . . . as to whether she would exericse it in these circumstances."[6] Since the family judged that a person in that situation would not want further care, a request to stop the respirator would be upheld.

Thus the court, in effect, ruled that doctors and families could stop treatment on a chronically vegetative patient, because it is reasonable to think that the patient, if competent and able to express a preference, would make the same decision. While it may be argued that a patient in a comatose state would choose, if able to speak, to go on living, the substituted judgment test need not be followed so strictly. When the person's interests are so slight that the concept of harm or benefit hardly appears to be relevant, the wishes of the family and society may appropriately be followed.

The *Quinlan* decision is likely to be followed by other courts. In the *Matter of Eichner*,[7] for example, New York trial and appellate courts used a theory similar to that used in *Quinlan*, to uphold their decision to disconnect a respirator on an eighty-year-old man who had suffered a cardiac arrest and subsequent brain damage during a hernia operation. The New York Court of Appeals affirmed, on different grounds, that there was clear evidence that the patient had previously, when competent, asked that his life not be prolonged if he ever ended up like Karen Quinlan. When proof of a prior wish to stop treatment on irreversibly comatose patients is absent, it is likely that courts in other states will follow *Quinlan*.

May treatment be stopped on incompetent patients who are terminally ill?

It depends. Terminal illness is a vague term that covers a range of illnesses and prognoses. A person can be terminally ill in the sense that he is suffering from an incurable illness, but may not die for months, or even years. In other cases of terminal illness death may be literally imminent and occur in a few hours or days. The important questions then, for determining when treatment can be stopped on an incompetent patient said to be terminally ill are: (1) how intrusive and painful the life-prolonging treatment is; (2) how long it will prolong the person's life; and (3) what the quality of that additional life will be. In some cases, the treatment will be so intrusive and painful, and the additional life it makes possible so impaired or painful, that one could reasonably say that judging from the patient's perspective, the treatment is not in his interest (hence, would not, under the substituted judgment test, be chosen by the patient if competent and able to speak). In such a case, treatment could legally be stopped, and indeed to provide it, could be said to violate the patient's right not to be treated.

In other cases, however, the extended life will be well worth the burdens that the treatment making it possible impose. In that case, treatment must be provided, regardless of the patient's future mental status and social worth, for it serves the patient's interest (hence, would be chosen by him under the substituted judgment test if the patient were competent and able to choose).

A case illustrating these principles is the *Saikewicz*[8] case from Massachusetts. Joseph Saikewicz, a severely retarded male (IQ about 15) of sixty-seven, who had spent most of his life in a state institution, was diagnosed as having acute myeloblastic monocytic leukemia, a cancer of the blood. Most adults in that situation would consent to a course of chemotherapy that would not cure the disease, but possibly prolong life for about four to thirteen months. Without chemotherapy, the patient would probably die within a few months.

The doctors sought court approval to withhold chemotherapy. The trial court agreed that treatment would not be in the patient's interest because it involved significant side effects and discomfort. The patient would not be able to understand what was happening to him, and would have to be forcibly restrained to have chemotherapy administered. The pain and suffering involved in the treatment would outweigh the benefit of a few additional months of life in such a state, and therefore was not in Saikewicz's best interest. The Massachusetts Supreme Judicial Court affirmed the decision. It applied the substituted judgment test and found that if Saikewicz were competent to express his preferences, he would, in light of his mental and physical prognosis, choose to reject therapy, because the pain, discomfort, and suffering of treatment would outweigh any possible benefits.

On the other hand, situations do arise in which a terminally ill incompetent person could benefit from treatment, which thus must be provided. Competent patients who are dying will often want life-prolonging treatment, at least for a while.

Patients who are incompetent might also have an interest in staying alive. This is most apt to be true where the patient might recover competency, or if permanently incompetent, is conscious, and able to relate to others. (It is unlikely where the terminally ill patient is comatose or severely brain damaged.) Relatively painless treatments that will allow incompetent patients to live for several weeks or months, would ordinarily be in their interest, just as it would be in the interest of a competent patient. For example, a mentally retarded person with cancer, has a right to surgery, chemotherapy, and radiation therapy, even if it will not prevent death. His right to treatment ends only when he no longer benefits from the treatment sufficiently to justify the pain and discomfort of the therapy.

A 1981 New York case shows that the courts will sometimes require treatment of a terminally ill incompetent patient.[9] John Storar, a profoundly retarded fifty-two-year-old man who had been institutionalized since he was five, suffered from an advanced stage of bladder cancer. He was treated with radiation therapy, but the cancer metastasized to his lungs, and the doctors estimated that he would die in two to six months. He also began losing massive amounts of blood, which necessitated blood transfusions every eight days. His mother, a seventy-seven-year-old widow, requested that the transfusions be stopped. They were painful, required physical restraints, and only prolonged the pain of his dying. The director of the facility in which he lived requested judicial approval for further treatment. The trial court found that "Storar's best interest will be served by terminating the transfusions and that this would be, . . . Storar's preference were he able to make a decision and articulate it,"[9A] and ordered the transfusions stopped. The New York Court of Appeals reversed the decision and ordered Storar to be treated. It found that the transfusions, which did not appear to involve excessive pain, would not cure the cancer, but would prevent a more immediate death from loss of blood. Any pain Storar would have to endure was thus justified by the continued life it made possible.

The court concluded its analysis:

Although we understand and respect his mother's despair, . . . a court should not . . . allow an incompetent patient to bleed to death because someone, even someone as close as a parent or sibling, feels that this is best for one with an incurable disease.[9B]

May treatment be withheld from an incompetent patient who is not terminally ill?

It depends. Under the principles of *Quinlan* and *Saikewicz*, incompetent persons cannot be denied medical care solely because they are mentally incompetent and experience a life that some people think lacks meaning. Treatment can be withheld from incompetent patients only when treatment will not be beneficial. Since incompetent patients generally are assumed to benefit from continued life without pain, it often will be in their interest to be treated and to go on living. As long as they retain consciousness they are legally entitled to the same care that competent patients in those circumstances would receive.

However, there are several situations in which the courts have found, or could find, that further treatment is not in the patient's interest, even if the patient were not terminally ill and could live indefinitely if the treatment were provided. One such situation, typified by the *Quinlan* case, is where the nonterminally ill incompetent patient is comatose, or so severely damaged that awareness of others is not possible. The courts are likely to rule that existence in such a diminished state serves no interests of the patient, and therefore under the substituted judgment and best interests tests could be omitted. Whatever the validity of this reasoning, courts faced with such situations are likely to follow *Quinlan* and *Eichner* and rule that further treatment is no longer in the vegetative patient's interest and can be omitted.

Where the non-terminal incompetent patient is conscious and likely to remain so, there will be far fewer situations in which non-treatment and an early death would appear to be in his interests. The strongest case for non-treatment would be if the patient's condition entailed such suffering that death were preferable, or if the life-prolonging treatment were itself painful and the life it made possible was of such poor quality that it could be reasonably said that the incompetent person, if able to choose, would forego additional life rather than undergo such treatment. A typical case presenting this issue is the question of when renal dialyses may be stopped on a retarded or senile person. Although dialysis requires two or three six hour treatment sessions a week, it is a treatment which many people tolerate for years. Given its capacity to prolong a person's life for months or years, in many cases it will be in the incompetent person's interest to receive it. [10]

Finally, incompetent patients facing amputation of gangrenous limbs may not be terminally ill, but may be reasonably found in some cases to have, from their own perspective, no further interest in life. Competent patients are generally free to reject amputation when in their judgment the resulting life is not a sufficient good to outweigh the burden of the operation and the resulting impairment. The courts have generally assumed that if the patient is incompetent, the amputation should be ordered, on the assumption that continued life is in the patient's interest. But if the substituted judgment or best interest test is properly applied, amputation should not necessarily be ordered. Amputation may not necessarily serve the patient's interest, because it will merely prolong living in a situation of pain, discomfort, and impairment that may outweigh, from the patient's perspective, any corresponding benefit from living. Or, amputation might be inconsistent with past expressions of how he wanted to be treated when incompetent, and there is no reason to think that he has changed that preference in a finding of incompetency. In the *Quackenbush* case, [11] for example, a finding of incompetency should not necessarily have led to an order for the amputation, because a nonambulatory life in a nursing home for Quackenbush could conceivably have caused him more harm than benefit.

In other situations, amputation could be found to serve the incompetent patient's interests and be chosen by him under the substituted judgment test if he were able to choose. As in all decisions concerning incompetent patients, however, courts must look at a situation from the patient's perspective. The inevitability of death, and the degree of patient awareness are important factors, but they do not automatically determine when treatment no longer serves the patient's interests.

May treatment be stopped on a critically ill person who is senile?

It depends. Many people think that at a certain stage of senility, life is no longer meaningful for the person or worthy of respect, and that necessary medical treatments can be stopped. Indeed, studies have reported that it is common practice in some hospitals and nursing homes, to withhold antibiotics and other necessary treatments from elderly patients.[12]

The legality of such practices, however, can be questioned under the principles outlined in this chapter. The key question is whether treatment is, from the patient's perspective, in her interest because of the prolonged life it makes possible and hence likely to be chosen if she were competent to choose. Senility, even chronic senility, does not necessarily mean that that person will not benefit from a prolonged life, and therefore that all medical treatment can be stopped. An elderly nursing home patient may have an interest in being treated with antibiotics for pneumonia, even though it will only allow her to exist some months longer in a state of senility.[12A] On the other hand, it may not be in her interest to have her life prolonged if the medical treatments essential to do so are extremely burdensome and painful.

The most recent guidance from the courts on how the substituted judgment test applies to senile patients, occurred in the *Spring* case.[13] Earle Spring, a seventy-eight-year-old man who had been an active outdoorsman, was chronically senile and living in a nursing home. He suffered from total kidney failure and had to be taken thrice weekly to a dialysis center for a six-to-eight hour session to purify his blood. Sometimes he became obstreperous and kicked the attendants and often had to be sedated or strapped down. His son petitioned to be appointed guardian to authorize that the dialysis be stopped. Without dialysis Mr. Spring would soon die; with it, he might have survived for as long as five years. The courts upheld the termination of dialysis on the ground that in the view of Spring's wife and son, he would if competent, have made the same decision.

This result is difficult to justify in terms of Spring's best interests, since the benefit to him of additional life would seem to outweigh the burdens of dialysis. The case shows the errors that can arise when decisions about incompetent patients are made indirectly through the substituted judgment test, rather than approached directly by focussing on the patient's best interests.

May doctors withhold nourishment and antibiotics from incompetent patients denied other forms of treatment?

It depends. Medical treatment, such as respirators, surgery, chemotherapy, and dialysis, may legally be stopped or withheld from incompetent patients on the ground that it is not in their interest. (Under the substituted judgment test discussed on p. 51, the patient, if he is competent to choose, would reject the treatment.) Withholding such treatments, however, may not always lead to the patient's death. Some patients will survive for long periods after seemingly essential treatments such as respirators are stopped, as occurred in the *Quinlan* case. An important question is whether other, less invasive forms of medical care, such as intravenous or nasogastric feeding and antibiotics, may also be stopped.

The courts have not yet ruled on this question, though murder charges have been brought against two Los Angeles physicians who ordered that all feeding and fluids be stopped on an irreversibly comatose patient who continued to live after his respirator was withdrawn.[14A] The answer will depend on how they apply the substituted judgment or best interests tests and assess the interests of patients in those situations. Under these tests it would probably be legal to stop feeding and antibiotic treatment if the prolonged life that treatment made possible was not in the patient's interest, as might occur if the patient were chronically vegetative or imminently dying. If further life, no matter how easily obtained, is not good for the patient, then any means that prolongs life, including nutrition and antibiotics, could be withheld.

On the other hand, if the basis for stopping treatment is its intrusive, painful, or burdensome nature, and not the mere fact of life extension, then medical treatments that do not impose those burdens, but could extend life, could not legally be withheld. Thus, nutrition and antibiotics, which ordinarily do not involve such burdens as to make the additional life they provide undesirable, would be legally required.

Unfortunately, the courts have not always made clear the precise basis of their nontreatment decisions—whether it was the harm from life extension itself, or the harm from the medical means utilized. In *Quinlan*, for example, it was not clear whether the respirator could be stopped because the chronic vegetative state that it made possible was itself a harm, or whether the burden and discomfort of total dependence on a respirator made any additional life worthless. However, the court did seem to emphasize the severe impairment of the comatose condition more than the burdens of the respiratory care.[14] If this reading of the case is correct, then nasogastric and intravenous feeding could also be legally stopped, for they allow the state of severe impairment to continue.

In other cases, however, such as *Saikewicz*[15] and *Spring*,[16] the decision appeared to be based on the burdens that the treatments in question entailed, and not merely the fact of continued existence. Since providing food and antibiotics usually do not entail such heavy burdens, it is unlikely that the courts would allow those forms of life-support to be withheld from Earle Spring or Joseph Saikewicz.

Do family members have a right to stop treatment on an incompetent patient?

No. Only a competent patient or a court-appointed guardian have a legal right to stop treatment. The doctor's duty to give or withhold care depends upon the rights of the incompetent person. If the treatment will be beneficial, the patient has a right to be treated. If the treatment will not serve the patient's interests, the doctor's obligation to treat ends. Ordinarily the doctor's assessment of these issues must be approved by the incompent patient's guardian or legal representative. The family has no independent rights of their own in the treatment decision.

Often, however, doctors regard the family as if it had the legal authority to decide on the treatment of the incompetent patient. Doctors may ask the spouse or next of kin to consent to decisions to give or stop treatments. If the family refuses, the doctor is not obligated to follow their wishes, and should determine what best serves the patient's interests, for the family has no right to harm an incompetent person. In one such case, a seventy-nine-year-old former banker, incompetent from senility, needed simple surgery to replace the battery in his pacemaker. His wife refused permission because "he knows nothing," has no memory, and he "is turning into a vegetable."[17] The trial judge correctly applied the applicable principles and appointed a guardian to authorize whatever treatment was "necessary to protect his health and life," since further life in his condition was *how?*

apparently in his interests, and the spouse had no right to prevent it.[18]

In another case, a blood transfusion was given over the objection of the husband of a Jehovah Witness because it could independently be determined that treatment was in the patient's interests.[19] There was evidence that the patient herself would not consent to a transfusion, but did not believe she would be damned if this was done. Since the treatment would provide a healthy normal life, it could be reasonably inferred that it would be in her interest. Similarly, in the *Storar* case (see p. 55), a mother's determination that her adult retarded son would not, if competent, choose to have blood transfusions replace blood lost due to bladder cancer, was overridden on the ground that the patient's interest would be best served by treatment.

Must the doctor get the consent of the family before treating or withholding care from an incompetent patient?

No. As the previous answer shows, such consent is not legally required, unless a relative has been appointed guardian of the patient and has the authority to decide on treatment. Where there is a guardian doctors should never act without getting the guardian's consent. In such cases, it is wise to inform the family of the situation as well, so that they may consult with the guardian or even challenge his decision if they think it does not serve the patient's interests.

Often, however, patients incapable of consenting will not be officially declared incompetent and have a guardian appointed. As a practical matter in those cases, rather than go through the formalities of having the patient be declared incompetent and appointing a family member as guardian, doctors will get the family's consent to stop treatment. The family's decision, however, is not legally binding on the doctor. If they refuse to give their consent, treatment can still be legally stopped if it is no longer in the interests of the patient. Similarly, treatment can still be legally provided over the family's objection if it will benefit the patient. However, when the family disagrees with the doctor's view of the patient's interests, the doctor should ask that a guardian be appointed and that a court approve any disputed medical decision. Although judicial approval is not legally required, it will minimize the possibility of suits and is generally advisable.

It is also important to recognize that family agreement with the doctor's decision does not automatically protect the doctor against legal liability (though it greatly reduces the chances of a suit). If the doctor's decision is challenged legally, as might occur in a criminal prosecution for unlawful termination of care or a civil suit on behalf of the deceased brought by a friend or a member of the family who disagreed with the course chosen, the legal effect of relying on the next of kin is unclear. The question will be whether the interests of the incompetent patient were reasonably protected. If they were not, then the consent of the family will not protect the doctor.[20] However, if the interest of the incompetent are unclear, and the doctor has consulted the next of kin to try to ascertain what is best, the courts may well find that the doctor has pursued a reasonable course of action and will not be held liable.

What if the family members disagree among themselves about the proper treatment of an incompetent patient?

If the incompetent patient has a guardian, family disagreement with the guardian's decision will have no legal effect. However, they could try to influence the guardian or even challenge his actions legally, claiming that they are not in the best interests of the patient.

If, as is more likely, no guardian has been appointed, the family has no legal right to make any decisions about the patient's treatment. Family disagreement over treatment should not stop the physician from making decisions that serve the interests of the patient. Practically speaking, however, in cases of disagreement, doctors should ask the courts to appoint a guardian and determine the patient's rights. A court faced with such a situation should focus on the interests of the incompetent patient and appoint a guardian most likely to protect them.

One such situation arose in the *Nemser* case.[21] Sally Nemser was an eighty-year-old widow living in a nursing home who suffered from heart disease, a stroke, and pneumonia. When her foot became gangrenous, her doctor recommended amputation to save her life. The woman did not want the operation, but, in her doctor's view, she did not understand the nature of the surgery and therefore was not competent to refuse. Her three sons disagreed over treatment. One, a doctor, objected to the surgery on medical grounds. The other two were in favor of it, and petitioned the courts to appoint them guardians to consent to the operation. The court found that Mrs. Nemser was incompetent, but refused to appoint a guardian to consent to the surgery, finding that because of the medical risks and low chances of success, amputation was not in her interests.

In another case, a nephew disagreed with the decision of a husband and son to go along with the refusal of a blood transfusion by a questionably competent Jehovah's Witness.[22] The patient had lost considerable blood from microcytic anemia and needed transfusions to stay alive. The court resolved the question by focusing on the interest of the woman. Finding that she was terminally ill and unlikely to live long even with the transfusion, the court refused to order the transfusion.

Must doctors and family go to court to stop treatment on incompetent patients?

No. Court approval is legally optional. Doctors, hospitals and families sometimes ask courts to decide whether they may stop treatment on incompetent patients. They do so to have a guardian appointed, to settle disputes among the family or between the doctor and family about the proper course of action, or to protect the doctors and hospital from legal liability. Since resort to the courts can have substantial costs for all parties, it should occur only when other alternatives for resolving the situation have failed.

In some instances, as a result of misunderstanding or uncertainty in the law, lawyers have advised going to court without sufficient reason to justify the resulting stress to patients and families. Some lawyers, for example, have interpreted the *Saikewicz* case as requiring doctors to obtain judicial approval to stop treatment. Yet no court has made judicial approval for terminating treatment mandatory, although some courts, such as those in Massachusetts,[23] have said that only a court can give a doctor legal immunity for his actions. (Massachusetts does require prior judicial approval for nontreatment decisions for institutionalized persons and wards of the state who have no family members willing to be involved in the decision.[23A])

Indeed, even the courts that have required judicial approval for advance immunity, have made it clear that court action is not always necessary.[24] The legality of stopping treatment depends upon whether the incompetent patient has a right to be treated, and not on whether a court has first approved the decision. This assessment depends, in turn, on whether the treatment will, from the incompetent patient's perspective, serve his interest, and hence satisfy the best interest or substituted judgment tests. If the family and doctors make the correct decision about the patient's interests, their actions do not become illegal just because a court has not approved it in advance.

However, advance judicial approval has certain advantages for all parties concerned. The assessment of the patient's best interest if he were competent is often complex, requiring information about, and trade-offs among, several factors. Resort to the courts might protect patients by assuring that their rights were properly understood and that decisions are made on an adequate factual basis. It may also assure doctors that they can give or stop treatment without fear of legal liability, and will eventually clarify the rules for nontreatment decisions. When doctors are uncertain about their obligations, or want to avoid risking legal liability, seeking judicial approval— though not legally required—might be the best course of action. In emergencies a prompt judicial decision with few of the formalities of typical court proceedings, can usually be arranged, though it can have substantial costs for the patient and family, and should not be done if there are reasonable grounds for the course of action chosen.

An example of an unnecessary use of the courts occurred in a New York case involving a 41-year-old diabetic who had lost his sight and both legs and wanted to stop the dialysis treatment keeping him alive.[24A] He was found competent by two psychiatrists, and with the approval of his family and religious advisors signed refusal of consent forms prepared by the hospital. Rather than accede to his request, however, the hospital sought a court order to continue treatment, apparently out of fear of legal liability After holding a hearing in the patient's room, the judge eventually ruled that the patient had a right to discontinue dialysis. Given the well-established right of a competent patient to refuse care, and in New York, under *Eichner*, to give permission in advance to stop treatment if he becomes incompetent, the hospital seemed to have no reasonable grounds for seeking court approval of the patient's decision. Their refusal to honor the patient's lawful request increased enormously the stress which the patient and family were experiencing. Going to court in such cases may even lead to suits against the hospital, since a disgruntled family could then sue the hospital for intentional infliction of emotional distress, or for battery and false imprisonment on behalf of the patient.

Must hospital ethics or prognosis committees approve decisions to stop treatment of incompetent patients?

It depends. Hospitals could institute review procedures for terminating care on incompetent patients which doctors, as a condition of employment or staff privileges, are obligated to follow.[25] Doctors who do not comply, could be disciplined or have their admitting privileges suspended. In addition, failure to consult a committee that is regularly consulted by other doctors, could be viewed as unprofessional conduct, and increase the chance of criminal or civil liability.

Legally, however, the courts have not required committee approval, though they have indicated that this could provide doctors with immunity from later suits. In the *Quinlan* case, for example, a doctor who turned off a respirator on a chronically vegetative patient could not be criminally or civilly liable if a hospital ethics or prognosis committee had first confirmed that there was "no reasonable possibility of Karen's ever emerging from her present comatose condition to a cognitive, sapient state."[26]

Although not legally required, hospitals and doctors can protect themselves, as well as their patients, by creating such committees. Given the uncertain legal status of many nontreatment decisions, the possibility of error and bias, and the sophisticated judgments required by the substituted judgment test, doctors and hospitals will be in a better position to defend public criticism and legal challenges if they have set up such committees. The committees need not have ultimate decision-making authority. They can be consultative, and resort to them made optional. A doctor who follows their advice will be on firmer legal ground in a later legal challenge than one who has acted on his own.

Can family members and doctors be sued for terminating treatment on incompetent patients?

Yes. However, liability will depend upon whether the action was legally justified. This would be a violation of the rights of incompetent patients if further treatment is in their interest and would be chosen by them if they were competent.

Legally, persons who withhold necessary medical care that they have a legal duty to provide, or who actively kill another, may be guilty of homicide, as well as be open to civil liability. Doctors have a legal duty to treat their patients as long as treatment will benefit them, and as long as they have not arranged for adequate alternative care. Family members may also have a legal duty to provide treatment or a duty not to interfere with, or prevent a doctor from treating the incompetent patient; otherwise, criminal charges for homicide could be levied against the family, doctors, and nurses. Civil liability for abandonment or wrongful death is also possible, though damages will usually be small and suits on this ground rare.

As a practical matter, however, it is highly unlikely, but not impossible, that criminal charges would be brought against doctors and families who discontinue the treatment of incompetent patients. Passive euthanasia of incompetent patients appears to be widespread in hospitals and nursing homes,[27] much of which may be unlawful because the patient still had an interest in living. However, with a few exceptions, no doctor or family has ever been prosecuted for stopping treatment on critically ill incompetent patients. Civil suits are also rare. However, the rarity of prosecution should not lead doctors and families to ignore its possibility. Suits may be rare because people are not aware of the extent of the practice, and no one is available to represent the deceased patient's interests. In more flagrant cases, suits, or even criminal charges, could be brought. For example, a nurse who disconnected several terminal patients from respirators was prosecuted for manslaughter in Baltimore.[28] She was not convicted because the jury believed her defense that the patient was already brain dead when the disconnection occurred. Had there not been evidence of brain death, she might have been convicted. In another case the Los Angeles District Attorney filed murder charges against two physicians who ordered all feeding stopped on a irreversibly comatose patient who had been taken off a respirator.[29]

Can doctors or families actively kill patients on whom treatment may be stopped?

No. The law does not permit active euthanasia even when the patient is competent and consents, and even when the patient will otherwise linger in a state of great suffering.[30] When the patient is incompetent and his wishes are unknown, the reasons against active euthanasia are all the stronger, for the possibility of mistake is greater. Even if treatment can be legally stopped because it is not in the patient's interest, and doctors may administer drugs to relieve pain that might, as a side effect, also depress respiration and hasten death, they may not actively kill a dying or critically ill incompetent patient in order to spare him from further suffering.

It is possible that killing incompetent patients by injecting drugs does occur in some cases, though its incidence is unknown and far lower than that of passive euthanasia of such patients. Doctors, as well as families and friends, might engage in the practice, usually for "humanitarian" reasons. Prosecutions have been rare, usually because it is done secretly, or is approved by those aware of it. When such cases do surface, prosecution usually occurs because many people disapprove of active killing. Prosecution, however, will not always lead to conviction. In the United States, doctors have been prosecuted for homicide on two occasions[30] for allegedly actively killing terminal patients (a few prosecutions have also occurred in Europe).[31] In one case, a doctor allegedly injected air bubbles, and in the other, potassium chloride, in order to kill terminal cancer patients who would soon expire anyway. Although the juries could have legally convicted the doctors if the patients were alive when the injections occurred, in both cases the doctors were acquitted. Similarly, in a 1981 Massachusetts case, a nurse was acquitted of homicide when she claimed that she had administered a lethal dose of morphine to a nonterminally ill cancer patient in good faith, according to a doctor's orders.[31A] On the other hand, persons who have drowned or suffocated a chronically ill family member have been convicted.[32]

Is euthanasia of incompetent patients ever legal?

It depends on how one defines euthanasia, the means used, and the situation of the incompetent patient. The term *euthanasia*, which literally means a good or happy death, usually refers to a decision to bring about a person's death earlier than would otherwise occur in order to benefit the patient. The legality of the practice depends upon whether the person's death is actively or passively caused, whether it is voluntary or involuntary, and whether death serves the patient's interests.

As this chapter has shown, passive euthanasia of incompetent patients by stopping essential medical treatments—a form of involuntary or nonconsensual euthanasia—sometimes is lawful and sometimes is not, depending on whether the benefits of treatment to the patient outweigh the burdens, and thus would be chosen by the patient if competent to choose. Active euthanasia, or directly killing an incompetent patient, is never lawful, even if passive euthanasia of the patient would be. The following chart summarizes the legal possibilities:

		PATIENT CONSENT	
		Voluntary	Involuntary
Type of	Active (Direct)	Illegal	Illegal
Means Used	Passive (Indirect)	Legal	May be Legal

NOTES

1. *In re* Quinlan, 70 N.J. 10, 355 A.2d 647 *cert. denied*, 429 U.S. 972 (1976); Superintendent of Belchertown v. Saikewicz, 373 Mass. 728, 370 N.E. 2d 417 (1977).
2. *Id.*
3. Robertson, *Incompetent Organ Donors and the Substituted Judgment Doctrine*, 76 Colum. L. Rev. 48 (1976).
4. *In re* Quinlan, .70 N.J. 10, 355 A.2d 647, *cert. denied*, 429 U.S. 972 (1976).
5. *Id.*
6. *Id.*
7. Eichner v. Dillon, 52 N.Y. 2d 363, 420 N.E. 2d 64, 438 N.Y.S. 2d 266 (1981).
8. Superintendent of Belchertown v. Saikewicz, 373 Mass. 728, 370 N.E. 2d 417 (1977).
9. In the Matter of John Storar, 52 N.Y. 2d 363, 420 N.E. 2d 64, 438 N.Y.S. 2d 266 (1981).
9A. *Id.* at 73.

9B. *Id.* A somewhat similar case arose before the Quinlan and Saikewicz cases in Florida in 1971. Mrs. Carmen Martinez, age seventy-seven, suffered from hemolytic anemia, a disease that destroys the red blood cells, and would die unless she would receive continuous transfusions. In order to do this, the doctors would have to open her veins surgically in a procedure called a cut-down. Both she and her daughter objected to the cut-downs and transfusions. The doctor went to court to determine his legal obligation. The judge found the patient incompetent, but appointed her daughter guardian with legal power to refuse treatment. The transfusions would postpone death only for a few weeks, and provided such a poor quality of life for the patient at such substantial cost, that they could be found, from the patient's perspective, not to be in her interests. See R. Veatch, *Death, Dying and the Biological Revolution* 116–17 (1976).

10. But see Matter of Spring, 405 N.E. 2d 115 (Mass. 1980).

11. *In re* Quackenbush, 156 N.J. Super 282, 383 A.2d 785 (1978).

12. Brown and J. Thompson, *Nontreatment of Fever in Extended-Care Facilities*, 300 N. Eng. J. Med. 1264–50 (1979).

12A. Collins v. Davis, 44 Misc. 2d 622, 252 N.Y.S. 2d 666 (Sup. Ct. 1964).

13. Matter of Spring, 405 N.E. 2d 115 (Mass. 1980).

14. *In re* Quinlan, 70 N.J. 10, 355 A.2d 647, *cert. denied*, 429 U.S. 972 (1976).

14A. "Doctors Face Murder Charges in Patient's Death," *Los Angeles Times*, August 19, 1982, p. 1, col. 4.

15. Superintendent of Belchertown v. Saikewicz, 373 Mass. 728, 370 N.E. 2d 417 (1977).

16. Matter of Spring, 405 N.E. 2d 115 (Mass. 1980).

17. Collins v. Davis, 44 Misc. 2d 622, 252 N.Y.S. 2d 666 (Sup Ct. 1964).

18. *Id.*

19. United States v. George, 239 F. Supp. 752 (1965).

20. See Karp v. Cooley, 493 F.2d 408 (1974), but *cf.* Nishi v. Hartwell, 52 Haw. 188, 473 P.2d 116 (1970).

21. Petition of Nemser, 273 N.Y.S. 2d 624 (1966).

22. *In re* Phelps, No. 459–207 (Milwaukee County Ct., filed July 11, 1972). For a summary of this case see R. Veatch, *Death, Dying and the Biological Revolution*, 120–21 (1976).

23. Superintendent of Belchertown v. Saikewicz., 373 Mass. 728, 370 N.E. 2d 417 (1977); Matter of Spring, 405 N.E. 2d 115 (Mass. 1980).

23A. Custody of a Minor, 385 Mass. 697, 702–10 (1982).

24. Matter of Spring, 405 N.E. 2d 115 (Mass. 1980). Eichner v. Dillon, 420 N.E. 2d 64 (1981) has reached a similar conclusion.

24A. "Diabetic Dies After L.I. Judge Stops His Life-Sustaining Care," *New York Times*, Oct. 23, 1982, p. 1, col. 4.

25. *Optimum Care for Hopelessly Ill Patients, a Report of the Clinical Care Committee of the Massachusetts General Hospital*, 295 N. Eng. J. Med., 315 (Aug. 12, 1976); Rabkin, Gillerman, and Rice, *Orders Not to Resuscitate*, 295 N. Eng. J. Med. 317 (Aug. 12, 1976).
26. *In re* Quinlan, 70 N.J. 10, 355 A.2d 647, *cert. denied*, 429 U.S. 972 (1976).
27. Brown and J. Thompson, *Nontreatment of Fever in Extended-Care Facilities*, 300 N. Eng. J. Med. 1264–50 (1979).
28. "Jury Votes Acquittal in Mercy-Killing Case of Nurse, 10–2," *Baltimore Sun*, Mar. 21, 1979, p. 1.
29. "Doctors Face Murder Charges in Patient's Death," *Los Angeles Times*, August 19, 1982, p. 1 col. 4.
30. R. Veatch, *Death, Dying and the Biological Revolution*, 78–80 (1976).
31. " 'Mercy-Death' Admission by Doctor Stirs Denmark," *The Boston Globe*, Aug. 9, 1974, p. 26.
31A. *New York Times*, Oct. 24, 1981, p. 10.
32. Commonwealth v. Nixon, 319 Mass. 495, 66 N.E. 2d 814 (1946); Repouille v. United States, 165 F.2d 152 (2nd Cir. 1947).

VI

The Right Not to Be Resuscitated

Most hospitals have specially equipped cardiopulmonary teams to resuscitate patients whose hearts have ceased functioning. When a patient's heart stops, the hospital loudspeaker will summon the team by the term *Blue Cart, Code 6*, or some other designation that tells the team where to go. Members of the team will rush to the bedside and begin resuscitation. Time is crucial, since irreversible brain damage can occur if oxygen is cut off from the brain for more than a few minutes.

The resuscitative team's efforts are expert, highly intrusive, and require sophisticated equipment. They typically involve cardiac massage, insertion of endotracheal tubes to provide oxygen, injection of medications into the heart or veins, defibrillators to give electric shocks to induce heart contractions, and similar measures. Immediate resuscitation may now save patients who in earlier years would have died. Resuscitation may also fracture bones, damage internal organs, and lead to long stays in intensive care units.

Because of the highly intrusive nature of these procedures, and the fact that they may merely restore the patient to continue an inevitable process of dying, doctors sometimes decide against resuscitation if an incompetent or terminal patient suffers cardiac arrest. A physician's decision not to resuscitate a patient is called an order not to resuscitate, sometimes referred to as a no-code, or no blue cart order. It will usually be communicated to nurses and other doctors caring for the patient, and for this purpose, may be written in

71

the patient's medical record. No-code orders have become a standard part of care of the critically ill. While few cases involving no-code orders have come to court, they concern the same issues that arise in the care of incompetent patients. This chapter discusses those issues.

Are orders not to resuscitate critically ill patients legal?

It depends. An order not to resuscitate is a decision to withhold care that could extend a patient's life. Its legality thus depends on whether the patient has a right to receive treatment. Since most patients in this situation will be incompetent at the time, their right to receive treatment will depend on whether it is in their interest to stay alive. (See Chapter V, The Right To Stop Treatment On Incompetent Patients). In many situations where no-code orders are written, the patient's prognosis and condition is so poor, that continued life and treatment, viewed from the patient's perspective, may not appear to be in her interest. Orders not to resuscitate such patients would be as legal as other non-treatment decisions. Indeed, they could be legally required where resuscitation would violate the patient's right not to be treated.

If the patient, on the other hand, has an interest in prolonging her life, then resuscitation is in her interest and would be legally required. In that case, the doctor who gave and the nurses and doctors who followed an order not to resuscitate, would deny the patient treatment that she had a right to have, and could be subject to criminal and civil liability. While suits or prosecutions are likely to be few, arbitrary or erroneous decisions could engender them. Doctors should thus use great care to assure that the patient not to be resuscitated, has no right to receive further treatment. He should follow hospital procedures, if any, for writing such orders, and seek the approval of any existing patient classification or review committees. In some cases resort to the courts may even be necessary.

In the Matter of Dinnerstein,[1] one of the few cases dealing with the legality of orders not to resuscitate, a distinction was made between patients who have a right to further treatment, and those who do not. Shirley Dinnerstein was a sixty-seven-year-old woman with Alzheimer's disease, an incurable, degenerative brain disease that typically leads to a vegetative or comatose condition. She also had suffered a massive stroke which totally paralyzed her left side. As the disease progressed, she was left in an essentially vegetative state, immobile, speechless, unable to swallow without choking, and barely able to cough. She was fed through a nasogastric tube, was catheterized and required bowel care, and suffered from high blood pressure. With vigorous care, she might have lived as much as a year, but she could suffer a cardiac or respiratory arrest at any time.

The patient's doctor recommended that if cardiac arrest occurred, the patient should not be resuscitated, and the patient's family (a daughter with whom she had been living, and a son who was a physician) agreed. In light of the legal uncertainty surrounding no-code orders, the doctor, hospital, and family, asked the courts to rule on the legality of the order. The Massachusetts Appeals Court held that an order not to resuscitate in these circumstances, was lawful, and that advance judicial approval was not necessary to write such orders. Resuscitation was not

> a treatment offering hope of restoration to normal, integrated, functioning, cognitive existence. . . .
> Attempts to apply resuscitation, if successful, will do nothing to cure or relieve the illnesses which will have brought the patient to the threshold of death.[2]

Another Massachusetts case also upheld a no-code order on the ground that it was not in the patient's interest to be resuscitated.[3] The case involved a five month old infant abandoned at birth who suffered from profound congenital heart and lung malformations and who had no hope of survival beyond a year. When the child was admitted to the hospital with a bacterial infection and placed on a respirator, his doctor recommended that a "no-code" be entered on the child's medical chart. The hospital sought authorization for the order from the juvenile court because his temporary guardian, the state Department of Social Services, refused to consent to the "no-code" order.

In a decision upholding the juvenile court's order that the "no-code" be entered, the Massachusetts Supreme Judicial Court found that a "full-code" order would involve a substantial degree of bodily invasion, pain and discomfort, and would do nothing but prolong the child's agony and suffering. It therefore would not serve the child's interest to be resuscitated, and would, if the child were competent to decide, be rejected by him. The court also upheld the juvenile court's refusal to change the "no-code" order when the doctors, after the child survived the bacterial infection, decided to with-draw it.

Must the guardian or family consent to an order not to resuscitate for it to be legally valid?

Not necessarily. Doctors involve families in no-code orders to varying degrees. In some cases, they might present the family with the situation and ask them to make a decision. It's more likely that they will inform the family of their decision and the reasons for it. Or they might write a no-code order in the patient's chart and tell the family nothing.

Legally, the same rules that apply to other treatment deci-sions for incompetent patients, apply here. Family members not appointed as a guardian, have no legal right to control the patient's care. If the patient has no right to be resuscitated because it is not in his interests, the guardian or family cannot, by refusing consent to the no-code order, legally command resuscitation. Similarly, family or guardian consent will not immunize a doctor from liability for a no-code order if resuscitation would be in the patient's interest.

As a practical matter, however, the best course of action for the doctor is to inform the family in advance and get their approval. The courts have not yet looked closely at no-code orders, and there is language in *Dinnerstein* suggesting that the wishes of the family are a controlling factor.[4] Notifying the family would also protect the patient's rights by giving the family a chance to object and bring about an authoritative determination of whether the order should be followed.

Must a doctor get the advance approval of a hospital committee or a court for no-code orders?

No. No court or state law has held that the advance approval of either a hospital review committee or a court is necessary to make a no-code order legal, if family members are willing to be involved in the decision. The *Dinnerstein* case specifically rejected advance judicial review, in such cases stating that the question

of what measures are appropriate to ease the imminent passing of an irreversibly, terminally ill patient in light of the patient's history and condition and wishes of her family . . . is not one for judicial decision, but one for the attending physician, in keeping with the highest traditions of his profession . . .[5]

However, the Massachusetts Supreme Judicial Court, in upholding a "no-code" order for a five-month old infant, did state that judicial review was required for institutionalized persons and wards of the state when a "loving family with whom physicians may consult" was absent. [5A]

As with other nontreatment decisions, failure to get advance approval will not in itself cause liability if a correct decision has been made. However, in cases where it is unclear whether the patient has a right to receive treatment, seeking judicial approval could clarify rights and duties, protect the physician, and prevent future disputes.

Nor has a review by a hospital committee of no-code orders been required by any court decision or state law. However, such approval could be required by the hospital as a matter of its own policy. In that case, a failure to follow the policy could affect the doctor's standing with the hospital. Failure to follow hospital procedures could also have legal consequences if a suit were brought against a doctor for wrongfully failing to resuscitate a patient for it might be evidence that the doctor has not followed professional standards for writing no-code orders. Thus, even though the courts have not yet required committee approval, doctors should seek the advice and approval of such committees if they exist. Indeed, it might be desirable to set up advisory committees to review difficult cases. Medical decisions to withhold care from incompetent patients that are subsequently challenged in a lawsuit, are likely to appear more reasonable and acceptable if they have been made in accordance with visible criteria and procedures that attempt to assure the patient's best interests.

Can a doctor be liable for not resuscitating a critically ill incompetent patient?

It depends. If resuscitation appears to be in the best interests of the patient and hence is his right, the doctor could be liable for wrongful death or even homicide. Thus, if she did order resuscitation, she could not be liable, even if the family objected. They have no independent right to control the patient's treatment and cannot have treatment in a patient's interest withheld.

A doctor could be liable, however, if she negligently assumes that resuscitation serves the patient's interest when it only prolongs his suffering. In that case, the doctor would be violating the patient's right not to be treated. A doctor could also be liable if the patient in a valid living will had requested no resuscitation, and the doctor knowingly violates the directive. However, no doctor has yet been sued for resuscitating a critically ill incompetent patient, and except in very flagrant cases of repeated, unjustified resuscitations, or refusal to follow a living will, such a suit is unlikely. In any event, damages for wrongful resuscitation beyond the costs of any additional medical care, are likely to be small.

What if resuscitation, if successful, would leave the patient in a brain-damaged or disabled state?

If the patient has a right to be resuscitated because she has a right to receive further care, doctors should not withhold it just because there is some chance that the patient will recover, though permanently brain damaged. The possibility of permanent brain damage enters into a determination of whether further care is required. If treatment is in the patient's interest, despite the possibility of brain damage or other impairment, a failure to resuscitate would violate the patient's rights.

If the patient is already brain damaged, or could survive resuscitation only in a brain-damaged state, there may be no duty to treat at all. In that case, a no-code order would be lawful, and indeed, required. If a doctor ignored this possibility, he could be sued for unnecessary treatment and the cost of the additional care.

It is important to remember that doctors cannot always accurately predict the patient's condition after resuscitation. Predictions about the degree of brain damage suffered during cardiac arrest are unreliable, and except for long periods with no cerebral oxygenation, should not be the basis for withholding resuscitation. For example, patients who ceased breathing for several minutes, have occasionally recovered.[6] If the resuscitated patient has suffered sufficient brain damage to justify nontreatment, then treatment can be omitted at a later period when the extent of the impairment and the prognosis are clearer.

Must a doctor get the consent of a competent patient to write a no-code order?

No. When the cardiac arrest does occur, the patient is likely to be incompetent. While a competent patient could legally give orders concerning resuscitation in the event that he became incompetent, the doctor has no legal obligation to ask a patient his wishes in advance. While many people might think it good practice to solicit the competent patient's views on this question, doctors might view such inquiries as a violation of standards of good care. One doctor stated in a leading medical journal that such questions "are thoughtless to the point of being cruel, unless the patient inquires, which he is extremely unlikely to do."[7] However, respect for competent patient's autonomy should mean that he be given the choice to decide before the need arises.

If the patient were competent at the time of cardiac arrest, then his wishes should control. However, a competent choice at that moment is not possible. A doctor who in good faith treated in such an emergency, could not realistically be found liable for battery.

Does a competent patient have a right to request no resuscitative measures if she becomes incompetent?

Yes. In those jurisdictions recognizing the validity of living wills, a competent patient may order that no resuscitation occur if she becomes incompetent. Depending on the jurisdiction, this directive would be binding on guardians, relatives, and doctors, and if ignored, could be a basis for a suit or disciplinary action against the doctor. In jurisdictions without living will legislation, a doctor could rely on such a directive as evidence of the patient's interests when she becomes incompetent. However, a doctor should not give an order not to resuscitate on the basis of a living will or prior directive if it would otherwise be in the patient's interest to be resuscitated. In that case, judicial clarification of the doctor's duty and the patient's right would be advisable (see chapter VIII).

How long must doctors try to resuscitate a patient who has had a cardiac arrest?

Resuscitation efforts should last as long as good medical practice dictates. Legally, as long as there is a reasonable chance that the resuscitative efforts will help the patient, they should continue. Thus, if doctors made only a sham or halfhearted attempt (called "partial codes" or "slow codes"), when more vigorous efforts would have rescued the patient, they could be criminally or civilly liable. (Such suits may be rare and proof difficult). As long as there is a duty to resuscitate because continued life is in the patient's interest, full resuscitative efforts should be made.

Must orders not to resuscitate be written in the patient's chart?

It depends. The law does not require that no-code orders be written in the patient's chart, though many hospitals have rules requiring written orders.[8] The Minnesota Hospital Association, for example, has adopted a policy requiring that no-code orders be written. Violation of such hospital policies would not lead to legal liability, but they could lead to loss of hospital privileges or other disciplinary actions against the doctor who fails to write the no-code order.

Doctors often prefer not to write a no-code order in the chart out of fear of legal liability, although verbal orders can also form the basis for liability. However, a written order, together with its rationale, could protect the doctor by showing that his actions were reasonably aimed at protecting the patient's and family's interests. In fact, a failure to enter a written order could increase the risk of suits for wrongful resuscitation. For example, if a nurse ordered resuscitation where it was not warranted in terms of the patient's interests, because the doctor had not complied with hospital policy for written no-code orders, the doctor would have been negligent and potentially liable for prolonging the patient's suffering and his additional medical expenses.

Must a nurse follow a doctor's no-code order if it is not written in the patient's chart?

It depends. Nurses are sometimes placed in a dilemma by doctors who verbally give no-code orders but who refuse to write it in the chart. A nurse who followed the doctor's verbal order, unless it appeared unwarranted, would not be criminally or civilly liable, though in a later suit a dispute could arise over whether the order had been given. She could, however, be disciplined by the hospital for violating its policy about no-code orders. Perhaps the best solution to his dilemma is to follow hospital policy and call the resuscitation team in all cases until a no-code order is written. It is most unlikely that a nurse who followed hospital policy rather than the doctor's verbal order, could be found liable for wrongful resuscitation.

Are "slow-codes" legal?

It depends. A "slow-code" or "partial code" is a charade in which the resuscitative team appears to be making maximum efforts to resuscitate. This ploy may be used when the family has not been informed of, or approved, a no-code order, or is present during a cardiac arrest and the doctors do not want to appear to be shirking their responsibilities. Although the practice is deceptive, its legality depends upon whether resuscitation is in the patient's interest and thus legally required. If resuscitation would benefit the patient, a slow-code violates the patient's right to receive treatment, and could lead to civil or criminal liability (suits are likely to be rare).

NOTES

1. In the Matter of Shirley Dinnerstein, Mass. App., 380 N.E. 2d 134 (1978).
2. *Id.* at 138–39.
3. Custody of a Minor, 385 Mass. 697 (1982).
4. *Id.* at 136, 139.
5. *Id.* at 139.
5A. Custody of a Minor, 385 Mass. 697, 709–710 (1982).
6. Southwick, and Dalglish, "Recovery After Prolonged Asystolic Cardiac Arrest In Profound Hypothermia: A Case Report and Literature Review," 243 J. Amer. Med. Assn. 1250 (1980).
7. Spencer *'Code' or 'No Code': A Nonlegal Opinion*, 300 N. Eng. J. Med. 138, 140 (1979).
8. Los Angeles County Department of Health Services' Hospitals, Guidelines for "No-Code" Orders, Appendix E.

VII

The Rights of Critically Ill Children

Ordinarily, parents will want the best treatment possible for a critically ill child, and doctors will try to give it. Sometimes, however, parents oppose essential medical treatments. They may object on religious or philosophical grounds; they might oppose blood transfusions or desire laetrile for a child with leukemia. Or, they may object to treatment when the child is born with handicaps—when a retarded child needs an operation to remove an intestinal blockage.

Such situations involve conflicts between parental desires, the rights and well-being of the child, and the wishes of the doctors involved. They are made more difficult by our strong tradition of deferring to parents on most matters of child rearing and the difficulty in being able to determine what best serves a child's interests. This chapter discusses the law that regulates the conflicts between a critically ill child, his family, and doctor.

Do critically ill children have a right to receive medical treatment?

Yes. They have the same right to receive necessary medical treatments from their doctors that other persons have. Every state imposes on parents (or guardians) a legal duty to obtain necessary medical care for children. A child who does not receive proper medical treatment is considered "neglected," and the state may intervene to protect the child.[1]

The child's right exists despite the parents' religious or philosophical beliefs about therapy, or their estimate of its efficacy. It also exists independently of IQ and mental status. (The mentally retarded or disabled child has the same right to

80

receive medical care from parents and doctors that the mentally healthy do.) If medical treatment will benefit the child,
it must be provided.

While the duty to maintain the health of the child is firmly
established, parents have some leeway to decide about treatment if it has such significant risks and dubious benefits, that
reasonable people could differ over its desirability.

In the *Hudson*[2] case, for example, the doctors recommended
the surgical removal of a grossly enlarged left arm of an
eleven-year-old girl, because it placed an extra burden on her
heart and caused psychological problems. The mother objected, and felt that the girl should be able to make up her own
mind when she was older. Since the operation had substantial
risk and was not lifesaving, the courts refused to find that the
child was neglected for want of medical care, and did not
order the operation.

In the *Sampson*[3] case, by contrast, the court ordered that
surgery be performed over parental objections to blood transfusions on a fifteen-year-old boy who had a massive deformity
of the right side of his face and neck (a neurofibromatosis).
This condition gave him a grotesque appearance and severely
affected his psychosocial development. The court found that
failure to correct the deformity so affected the child's welfare,
that despite substantial risk in the operation, it would not
allow the parental wishes to control.

Does a child have a right to receive medical treatment if the parents object on religious grounds?

Yes. While the right of parents to raise their children
according to the dictates of their conscience is treated with
great deference, it is well established that the welfare of the
child is paramount. Parents cannot prevent children from
receiving necessary medical care that would impair their
well-being or prevent them from surviving to an age where
they can decide for themselves, even if the parents have the
right to refuse such care. If the question of harm, however, is
one over which reasonable people may differ, the courts are
unlikely to intervene.

This issue arises most frequently with Jehovah's Witnesses
who object to blood transfusions for their children. The courts
have consistently ordered transfusions when the evidence
shows that the child's life or health will be endangered by the
refusal.[4] A typical case arose when Jehovah's Witness parents

refused to permit blood transfusions to be given to their twelve-year-old daughter who was suffering from erythroblastic anemia, a potentially fatal blood disease.[5] The court ordered the transfusion, pointing out that:

> The right to practice religion freely does not include the liberty to expose . . . a child . . . to ill health or death. Parents may be free to become martyrs themselves. But it does not follow they are free, in identical circumstances, to make martyrs of their children before they have reached the age of full and legal discretion when they can make that choice for themselves.[6]

May parents have a sick child treated with laetrile, vitamins, or other nonconventional therapies?

Probably not. Parents who object to conventional cancer therapy for children because of its side effects, or their beliefs in other therapies, have no right to choose treatments which will harm the child. Since there are effective therapies for many childhood cancers, such as leukemia, and increasing evidence that laetrile and vitamin therapy may themselves be harmful, it is likely that the courts will intervene and order standard therapy.

The highly publicized *Chad Green* case[7] from Massachusetts shows how the courts are likely to deal with such cases. Chad, at the age of twenty months, was found to have acute lymphocytic leukemia, a cancer of the blood. An aggressive program of chemotherapy administered over three years in three distinct phases, will bring about remission of the disease in nearly all cases, and five-year survival in fifty to seventy percent of children treated. The parents began the first course of chemotherapy which soon brought the disease into remission. A few months later, the parents stopped Chad's medication and the leukemia recurred. Since he would probably have died within six months without the drugs, the doctor sought court authority to treat him. A temporary guardian to consent to treatment was appointed, and the parents appealed. The Massachusetts Supreme Judicial Court denied their appeal on the ground that

> The evidence supported the judge's finding that the parents' refusal to continue with chemotherapy amounted to an unwillingness to provide the type of medical care

which was necessary and proper for their child's well-being. Where, as here, the child's very life was at stake, such a finding is sufficient to support an order removing legal custody from the parents, even though the parents are loving and devoted in all other respects.[8]

The state's interest in the welfare of children, the preservation of life and the ethical integrity of the medical profession, and the child's interest in continued survival (which outweighed the discomfort of the chemotherapy), justified the restriction on parental autonomy in deciding medical care for their child.

After the parents lost their appeal, they asked for legal authority to supplement the court-ordered chemotherapy with a program of "metabolic therapy" involving the daily administration of enzymes, large doses of vitamins, and laetrile. After an extensive evidentiary hearing on the question, the courts prohibited it. It found that the "metabolic therapy" was ineffective in the treatment of acute lymphocytic leukemia, poses a serious risk of injury to the child, and was therefore neither consistent with good medical practice, nor in the best interests of the child.[9]

It is possible, however, that parents would have more leeway to reject conventional therapy if they substitute a treatment that is accepted by a minority of licensed doctors. *In the Matter of Hofbauer*,[10] an eight-year-old boy was suffering from Hodgkin's disease, a disease almost always fatal if untreated, but which can be successfully controlled with radiation and chemotherapy. The parents rejected the doctor's recommendation for chemotherapy, and took their son to Jamaica, where he received nutritional and metabolic therapy that included laetrile. When they returned to New York the county social welfare department started proceedings to have the child removed from the parents' custody for treatment.

The New York Court of Appeals upheld the lower court's refusal to find the child to be neglected. The parents were obtaining care for their child from a licensed physician. Two doctors testified that the nutritional therapy was effective. The attending physician thought the child was responding well. In addition, both the father and doctor agreed to seek conventional therapy if it became necessary. In the court's view, this constituted "reasonable efforts to ensure that acceptable medical treatment is being provided their child,"[11] and foreclosed a finding of neglect. This decision, however, is limited to the narrow facts before the court, and does not constitute approval of laetrile and other nonstandard therapies in other contexts.

What happens if parents refuse to provide medical treatment for critically ill children?

Doctors, nurses, or other persons aware of the child's need for treatment, may ask the courts to assume temporary custody of the child and appoint a guardian to make decisions about medical care. The parents will have a hearing on whether the child is neglected or in need of protection because he is being denied necessary medical care. (A typical statute defines a neglected child as one "whose physical condition has been impaired or is in imminent danger of becoming impaired as a result of the failure of his parents . . . to exercise a minimum degree of care in supplying the child with adequate . . . medical care.")[12]

If the parents are not providing needed medical care, a guardian can be appointed to make medical care decisions for the child; the child can be placed in foster care; or parents can lose custody of the child. In some cases, nurses, doctors, or child welfare officials, may be given the right to come into the home to examine and treat the child, or the parents can be ordered to take the child to doctors for periodic examinations and treatment. Failure to comply with the court's protective orders would be punishable with either a fine or imprisonment.

If the child suffers injury or death as a result of the parents' failure to provide necessary medical care, the parents can be prosecuted for child abuse, neglect, or in extreme cases, homicide. The sincerity of parental religious and philosophical beliefs is no defense. For example, as far back as 1903, a father was convicted of manslaughter for allowing his infant daughter to die of pneumonia after he refused, on religious grounds, to obtain medical services.[13]

Does an infant born with serious mental and physical disabilities have a right to be treated?

Yes, as much as any other child or person. The child's right to be treated does not depend on his IQ, physical abilities, or social potential.[14] Aside from a few very extreme cases in which, from the child's perspective, the burdens of treatment outweigh the benefits, children with physical and mental handicaps have the same right to receive medical treatment that nonhandicapped children have. The fact that they appear from the perspective of "normal" people, to face a meaningless or greatly limited life, is not sufficient grounds for denying them essential medical treatments.

Do parents and doctors break the law if they withhold necessary medical treatments from handicapped children?

Yes. Infants with congenital defects such as Down's syndrome, meningomyelocele, and other severe impairments, are often denied essential treatments with the intent and result that they die.[15] The parents who refuse necessary treatments for such children are violating the child's right to receive medical treatment and could be criminally prosecuted. Failure to provide necessary medical care would constitute child abuse or neglect.[16] In addition, since it causes the child's death, and the parents have a legal duty to provide such care, it would also constitute homicide and they could be prosecuted for murder or manslaughter.[17] While parents of retarded children have been convicted for directly killing them,[18] there has been only one prosecution of parents and doctors for nontreatment of defective newborns. This case arose in Danville, Illinois, in 1981, after Siamese twins joined at the waist, were not treated or fed. The child welfare authorities intervened and obtained temporary custody. Soon after, the district attorney filed charges of attempted murder against the parents and doctors. The charges were dismissed at a preliminary hearing when no one testified that the parents and doctors actually ordered starvation.[18A] In retrospect, the case was not a strong one for prosecution. Prosecution should be reserved only for egregious cases where the interests of the child are much more clear-cut than here. Given the strong feelings many groups have about the sanctity of life, parents and doctors should be aware of the potential legal liability that could result if nontreatment decisions ignore the child's interests.

Do hospitals break the law if they allow parents and doctors to withhold necessary care from handicapped children?

Yes. Hospitals, like physicians and nurses, have a legal duty to protect patient welfare. Hospitals, for example, can be liable to patients injured by physician malpractice which the hospital could reasonably have prevented by limiting the physician's staff privileges.

Hospitals in which handicapped newborns are denied necessary treatments can be held legally accountable in several ways. If hospital officials have directly participated in an unjustified nontreatment decision, they can be criminally liable for conspiracy, homocide or child abuse, either as a principal or an accessory. If the hospital has not directly participated, it could be liable for failing to take steps to protect handicapped patients. However, the mere failure to regulate nontreatment decisions would probably not lead to criminal or even civil liability until custom or hospital licensing and accrediting agencies require that hospitals adopt guidelines and procedures for withholding treatment.

Perhaps the biggest danger to hospitals from exercising no supervision over nontreatment decisions is a loss of federal funds. In reaction to the Infant Doe case in Bloomington, Indiana (See p. 88) the Secretary of Health and Human Services in May, 1982 notified hospitals receiving federal funds that withholding of necessary medical treatment from handicapped children could constitute unlawful discrimination under Section 504 of the Rehabilitation Act of 1973 and lead to a cut-off of federal funds.[18B] Given the difficulty in knowing when nontreatment constitutes unlawful discrimination, hospitals should adopt guidelines that doctors must follow in stopping treatment on sick or handicapped children. If the guidelines require a finding that treatment is not in the child's interest and review by an ethics committee, it is unlikely that decisions made pursuant to them will cause legal problems.

Will the courts order treatment of handicapped children if the parents refuse to consent?

It depends on whether the case is brought to their attention. In many instances nothing will happen. The doctors will agree with the parents, and treatment will be withheld, usually leading to the death of the child. The child, however, may linger for days, months, or even years, in a more disabled state than if treatment had occurred. Although nontreatment violates the child's right to receive necessary care, the death will be listed on the death certificate as occurring from natural causes, and the matter will usually end there.

If the doctors disagree with the parents' refusal, or are

uncertain about their legal liability, they may ask a court to decide the question. This action will take the form of a declaratory judgment, or a petition to have a temporary guardian appointed to consent to medical care on the ground that the parents are neglecting the child.

An example of how the courts will handle such cases is *Maine Medical Center* v. *Houle*.[19] A child was born blind, with no left ear, nonfused vertebrae, and possible brain damage. She also had a tracheal-esophageal fistula (an opening between the windpipe and esophagus that prevents food from getting to the stomach), that would cause her death if not repaired. Both the parents and physicians wanted to withhold treatment because "probable brain damage has rendered life worth not preserving."[20] The hospital, however, was unsure of its legal position and asked the courts for permission to withhold care. The judge refused to allow the child's predicted poor quality of life to be considered. It ruled that the only issue was the medical feasibility of the procedure. If an otherwise healthy child who needed the surgery would have it done, then the fact that a child is blind, deaf, and/or retarded, is not an adequate ground for denying treatment.

Another example of court-ordered treatment is a Massachusetts case, *In the Matter of Kerri Ann McNulty*.[21] A month-old child suffering from congenital rubella, had congenital heart failure, respiratory problems, deafness, cataracts of both eyes, and was probably retarded. Her father wanted the respirator necessary to keep her alive stopped, and refused to consent to cardiac catherization and surgery which the surgeons thought necessary if she were to live for more than a few weeks. He considered these to be "extraordinary or heroic" life-supporting measures. The court refused to allow the child's handicaps to control, and appointed a guardian to consent to the operation.

Courts have also ordered treatment in cases of meningomyelocele, or spina bifida, a disease in which the child is born with an unclosed spinal column, and which may lead to paralysis of the lower limbs, hydrocephalus, bowel and bladder incontinence, and mental retardation. If operations to close the opening, or to insert shunts to drain off cerebrospinal fluid and other measures are not done, the child will almost certainly die. With treatment, the child may live for a long time with a range of physical and mental handicaps. A New York case involving such a child, arose when the parents refused consent for surgery to close the lesion on the back, and insisted on taking the child home to "let God decide if the child is to live or die."[22] At the time, the extent of the child's handicaps from the meningomyelocele were not known. However, since the lesion was very low on the spinal column, it appeared likely that she could be ambulatory with braces, and would have normal intellectual development, though she would have no bowel or bladder control and might need a cranial shunt in case of hydrocephalus. The doctors and hospital asked the court to appoint a guardian to consent to surgical repair of the back. The court ordered the treatment, finding that the child "has a reasonable chance to live a useful, fulfilled life," and that "a child born with handicaps [must] be given a reasonable opportunity to live, to grow and hopefully to surmount those handicaps."[23]

Recently, a few courts have deviated from the tradition of protecting the life of the handicapped child. Both cases involved fairly routine surgical procedures on children with Down's syndrome. Since persons with Down's syndrome may be only mildly or moderately retarded, are educable and may be able to do sheltered work, and live happy lives, it is very difficult to justify nontreatment as serving their interest. These cases have been widely criticized, and will probably not be influential as precedents.

The "Infant Doe" case arose in April 1982 when a baby boy was born with Down's syndrome and a trachael-esophagal fistula in Bloomington, Indiana.[23A] The parents refused to allow intravenous feeding and surgery to repair the esophagus. The hospital sought a court hearing to determine the legality of the parents' action. A juvenile court judge ruled that the parents could refuse the surgery and thus cause the child's death. The Indiana Supreme Court summarily affirmed without opinion. The baby died before an appeal could be taken to the U. S. Supreme Court. From the facts that are known (the hearing was closed and the judge issued no opinion), the case appears to elevate inappropriately, the parents' interest in having the child die immediately (rather than be adopted or raised in an institution) over the child's interest in life.

The *Becker* case,[24] a decision by an intermediate appellate court in California, also is difficult to justify in terms of the child's interest. Phillip Becker is a twelve-year-old boy mildly retarded as a result of Down's syndrome. His IQ is about 60;

he is educable, can communicate verbally, tend to many of his needs, is a member of a boy scout troop, and can work in a sheltered workshop setting. His parents never took him home after his birth, though they visited him occasionally in the private group residence in which he lives. His living expenses are paid for by the state of California.

A routine medical examination revealed that Phillip was suffering from a ventricular septal defect, a not uncommon defect that involves a hole between two chambers of the heart. If the hole is closed, he will have normal longevity. If it is not repaired, he will slowly deteriorate over the next five to ten years, with the heart forced to work harder, eventually pumping unoxygenated blood through the body. During the latter course of the illness he will be unable to engage in minimal exertions such as walking, will be gasping for breath, and eventually die from lack of oxygen.

Although advised of this possibility, the parents refused to give their consent to the operation. The persons caring for him informed the state child welfare authorities, who brought a petition asking that he be found neglected and that a guardian be appointed to consent to the surgery. After a hearing before a trial judge, the judge rejected the petition. On appeal to the California intermediate appellate court, the Court of Appeals, this decision was affirmed.[25] Petitions for discretionary further review to the California and United States supreme courts, were rejected.[26]

The *Becker* decision is poorly reasoned, and is unlikely to be followed by other courts that consider the issue. (Indeed, it has binding effect only within the fourth appellate district of California—the San Jose area). Although there is a five percent risk of mortality from the surgery, and postoperative complications are more likely than in the case of a normal child,[27] it is difficult to argue that the operation is not in Phillip's interest. Without it, he is certain to die a slow, painful death in the next five to ten years, with the last years full of agony and suffering. With it, he is assured a long life of ordinary health. Although the surgical risk is significant, it is not so high that reasonable people would reject the operation. Indeed, it is widely recognized that if Phillip had normal intelligence, the operation would clearly be seen to be in his interests.

The parents stated that they opposed the operation because they thought it would be better if he did not have his life extended. They were concerned that he might be placed in a state institution after their deaths. Unless life in an institution was so horrible that death were preferable, the parents' concern would not justify denying him such a necessary medical procedure. Nor is the risk of the surgery so great relative to the benefits that the decision should be left to parental discretion.

It seems that neither the parents, nor the court, in this case gave due regard to the interests of the child, and instead were swayed by uncritical scrutiny of claims of parental autonomy, and perhaps prejudice against the retarded. Unless the retarded are to be given fewer rights to life than other persons, the decision is unsupportable and should not be followed by other courts.[27A]

Must the doctor treat handicapped children when the parents refuse consent?

Yes. Once the doctor undertakes to treat the child, he has a duty to protect his patient and cannot, unless he arranges alternative equivalent care, withhold treatments essential for the child's well-being. This is true even if the parents object.[28] If the situation is an emergency, the doctor will have a duty to treat the child without parental consent. In nonemergency situations, the doctor should seek judicial approval for treating, or bring the matter to the attention of the child welfare authorities, who may then ask the courts to intervene. Child abuse reporting laws would independently require reporting, since parental neglect of basic medical care would constitute child abuse.

The doctor who goes along with the parents and takes no steps to protect the child, would be violating a legal duty to his patient, and could be prosecuted for violation of the child abuse reporting laws, or for child neglect. In cases where the child dies, he could also be prosecuted for homicide, for he has a legal duty to provide care once he has undertaken to treat the child, a duty that is not extinguished by the parents' refusal.[29]

As a practical matter, however, a doctor who acquiesces in the parental decision is unlikely to be prosecuted, though increased public attention to these matters could change things. Other than the Danville, Illinois Siamese twins case, the only reported prosecution of a doctor for withholding treatment from a newborn occurred in *Commonwealth* v. *Edelin*,[30] in the special context of abortion. Dr. Kenneth Edelin was convicted of manslaughter for failing to resuscitate a possibly viable infant that he had surgically removed from the mother as part of a lawful abortion. On appeal, the court upheld the legal theory of the conviction, but reversed on evidentiary grounds.

If the child is treated against the parents' wishes, who pays for it?

The parents. They are legally obligated to provide necessary medical care to their children and are responsible for the medical bills, even if they objected to treatment. Health insurance will cover some of the costs (many states have laws prohibiting the exclusion of congenital defects in health insurance policies).[30] If insurance is unavailable, most states have programs to share the costs of a disabled child so that the cost may end up being borne by the taxpayers.

Are parents required to keep and care for severely disabled children at home?

No. They are obligated to provide the child with necessary food, clothing, shelter, and medical care, but can fulfill this obligation by arranging for other persons, such as an institution, to provide this care. In many states[31] they may also be able to divest themselves of parental obligations by terminating the parental relationship. If foster or adoptive parents cannot be found, the children will remain under the custody of the state in an institution. While such institutions may be deplorably underfunded, life in the institution may, from the child's perspective, still be superior to no life at all. Although termination of parental rights and institutionalization is not an ideal solution, it does reconcile the child's interest in life, with the parents' interest in avoiding the burdens of caring for such a child.

May parents ever refuse life-saving treatment for a child?

Yes. Parents may refuse medical treatments that are not, from the child's own perspective, in his interests. Since the child is incompetent, his choice would be inferred through application of the best interests or substituted judgment tests.[32] Under these tests, those treatments may be omitted which are excessively burdensome in light of the benefits. This assessment involves weighing the child's diagnosis and prognosis, the burdens of treatment alternatives, and the length and quality of life that treatment provides. As with adult incompetents, treatment could be omitted on this ground in several different situations.

One would be where the child is in a chronically vegetative state and is unlikely ever to recover consciousness. A typical case of this kind arose in Los Angeles when a three-year-old was hit by a car and became irreversibly comatose.[33] Doctors and parents asked a court for permission to remove the child from a respirator. The court granted permission because the patient suffered "irreversible brain damage and is comatose and there is no possibility of his ever regaining consciousness."[34] The benefit to the child of continued existence in this state was so small, that the respirator could be legally shut off.

A second situation is where the child is terminally ill and will die no matter how aggressive the treatment. Burdensome treatments which merely prolong the dying process need not be provided. A child terminally ill with bone or blood cancer need not be treated with antibiotics or be resuscitated after a cardiac arrest if she would die anyway in a few days. The additional time may be too painful, or the treatments too burdensome.

The third situation of this sort might arise when a baby is very premature and is unlikely to live beyond a few weeks or months even with the best available neonatal intensive care. Although there is an initial duty to treat such children, a point may be reached when the child's interest, in light of the burdens and benefits of therapy from the child's own perspective, do not require treatment.[35]

On the other hand, a case where treatment would probably be legally required, arose when a two-year-old child suffered third-degree burns over eighty percent of his body in a fire.[36] The hospital to which he was admitted had to decide whether to transfer him to a specialized burn unit in another state. Without the transfer he was unlikely to survive. With it, the doctors estimated that he had a five percent chance of survival, but his legs and arms would have to be amputated, and his face would be severely scarred for life. His life would be spent in a wheelchair, with prosthetic devices for arms and hands. Under the best interests or substituted judgment tests, the question would be whether treatment, viewed from the child's perspective, would serve his interest in living and thus would be chosen if he were competent to decide. Applying this test, it seems more likely that transfer to the unit would be found to be in his interest and thus required, because the benefits and joys of being alive would outweigh the disadvantages of his physical disabilities. His mental ability was not impaired, and it is likely that he would be able to make the adjustments necessary for a meaningful life. Neither the doctors nor the parents could then legally refuse to transfer him to the special burn unit.

What should parents do if doctors insist on treatments which the parents want stopped?

Parents have the right to have unnecessary treatments, or treatments that are too burdensome in light of the benefits, stopped. However, they have no right to stop treatments that are in the child's interest. The doctor in such a case is legally required to take steps to protect the child.

It is usually not easy, however, to know when the point where treatment is no longer in the child's interests, is reached. Doctors might claim a moral and legal duty to protect the child, suggest that the parents are ignoring the child's interests, and threaten to get a court order if the parents continue to refuse. Differing perceptions of the child's interest among doctors, nurses, and parents can increase the stress of the situation and lead to disputes. The parents, however, may disagree and think that their child's suffering is being needlessly prolonged for the benefit of the doctors. Misunderstanding of the facts, miscommunication, and mishandling by the medical staff, can exacerbate the problem.[37]

Where parents disagree with the doctor's insistence on treating, they can demand complete information about their child's illness, its likely prognosis, and the risks and benefits of proposed and alternative treatments. If they have doubts about whether they are receiving the complete picture, they can insist on seeing the medical record,[38] and consult a physician not involved in the case. If disagreement still exists and the doctors insist on actions contrary to the parents' wishes, they can get a lawyer to protect their rights and initiate judicial proceedings.

Do critically ill children have a right to refuse necessary medical care?

Probably, if they are mature enough to understand the need for the medical procedure and the consequences of refusing.

In the past, minors had no right to determine their own medical care, but this rule has been gradually replaced by a recognition of the ability of mature, or emancipated minors, to consent to medical care.[39] Supreme Court decisions upholding the right of mature minors to terminate a pregnancy or have access to birth control without parental consent, suggest that mature minors may also have constitutional right to determine their own medical care that includes the right to refuse necessary medical treatment.[40] Thus, the constitutional right to refuse medical treatments recognized for adults, is likely to extend to minors as well.

While the courts have not yet faced this issue, the question could arise in two situations. One is where a critically ill teenager refuses further treatments and wants to die, but the parents want treatment. The second would be where both the child and parent oppose treatment, but the doctors or state disagree. In both cases, the outcome would depend on the child's condition and prognosis, the burdens and benefits of treatment, and the child's maturity and understanding of the situation. If the child were terminally ill and treatment would only prolong an imminent death, a situation in which adults have the right to refuse care, the courts would be likely to respect his choice.

On the other hand, where treatment would allow a child with severe handicaps to live, the courts may be more inclined to override a mature minor's refusal to be treated by raising doubts about his competency, or by holding that the state has a much lower burden to meet to justify instrusions on mature minors than on adults. A court, for example, may not uphold the right of a fifteen-year-old Jehovah's Witness to refuse an essential blood transfusion. Similarly, a sixteen-year-old girl who broke her neck in a diving accident and is paraplegic, might be treated against her will, even several months after the accident had occurred.

NOTES

1. Wald, *State Intervention on Behalf of 'Neglected' Children: A Search for Realistic Standards*, 27 Stan. L. Rev. 985 (1975).
2. *In re* Hudson, 13 Wash. 2d 673, 126 P.2d 765 (1942).
3. *In re* Sampson, 65 Misc. 2d 658, 317 N.Y.S. 2d 641 (Fam. Ct., Ulster Co., N.Y., 1970).

4. People *ex rel*. Wallace v. Labrenz, 411 Ill. 618, 104 N.E. 2d 769 (1952); State v. Perricone, 37 N.J. 403, 181 A.2d 751 (1962).

5. Morrison v. State, 252 S.W. 2d 97 (1952).

6. *Id*. at 103.

7. Custody of a Minor, 379 N.E. 2d 1053 (1978).

8. *Id*. at 1065.

9. Custody of a Minor II, 378 Mass. 712, 393 N.E. 2d 836 (1979).

10. 47 N.Y. 2d 648, 419 N.Y.S. 2d 936 (1979).

11. *Id*. at 941.

12. New York Family Court Act, § 1012.

13. People v. Pierson, 68 N.E. 243 (1903).

14. Robertson, *Involuntary Euthanasia of Defective Newborns: A Legal Analysis*, 27 Stan. L. Rev. 213 (1975).

15. Duff and Campbell, *Moral and Ethical Dilemmas in the Special-Care Nursery*, 289 N. Eng. J. Med. 890 (1973).

16. Robertson, *Involuntary Euthanasia of Defective Newborns: A Legal Analysis*, 27 Stan. L. Rev. 213 (1975).

17. *Id*.

18. Commonwealth v. Nixon, 319 Mass. 495, 66 N.E. 2d 814 (1940).

18A. Robertson, "Dilemma in Danville," The Hasting's Center Report, Oct. 1981, pp. 5–8.

18B. See 29 U.S.C. 794; 45 C.F.R. 84.3 (j); 45 C.F.R. 84.52.

19. Maine Medical Center v. Houle, Sup. Ct. Civil Action No. 74–145 (Cumberland Co. Me. 1974).

20. *Id*. at 4.

21. In the Matter of Kerri Ann McNulty, Probate Ct., No. 1960, Essex Co., Mass., Feb. 15, 1978.

22. Application of Cicero, 421 N.Y.S. 2d 965 (1979).

23. *Id*. at 967.

23A. *Newsweek*, Apr. 26, 1982, p. 59; *New York Times*, Apr. 17, 1982, p. 7; *Washington Post*, Apr. 18, 1982, p. 16.

24. *In re* Phillip B., 92 Cal. App. 3d 796, 156 Cal. Rptr. 48 (1979).

25. *Id*.

26. *In re* Phillip B., 92 Cal. App. 3d 796, 156 Cal. Rptr. 48 (1979), petition for rehearing denied, Cal. (July 19, 1979), *cert. denied*, (U.S. Mar. 31, 1980) (No. 79–698).

27. *In re* Phillip B., 92 Cal. App. 3d 796, 156 Cal. Rptr. 48 (1979).

27A. Since the decision another court has awarded guardianship of Phillip to a couple who had been caring for him, and it is possible that the surgery will eventually be done. Guardianship of Phillip Becker, Superior Court, Santa Clara County, Cal., No. 10198 (Aug. 7, 1981).

28. Robertson, *Involuntary Euthanasia of Defective Newborns: A Legal Analysis*, 27 Stan. L. Rev. 213 (1975).

29. *Id*.

30. 371 Mass. 497, 359 N.E. 2d 4 (1976).

31. Robertson, "Discretionary Nontreatment of Defective Newborns," in *Genetics and the Law*, eds. Annas and Milunsky, 450, 457 (1976).

32. Custody of a Minor, 379 N.E. 2d 1053, 1065 (1979).
33. In the Matter of Benjamin, Minor, Sup. Ct., Los Angeles Co., Cal., No. J914419, Feb. 15, 1979. See also In the Matter of Vincent Martin Young, Sup. Ct., Orange Co., Cal., No. 100863, Sept. 11, 1979.
34. *Id.* at 5.
35. Stinson, *On the Death of a Baby*, Atlantic (July 1979).
36. Author's personal observation.
37. Stinson, *On the Death of a Baby*, Atlantic (July 1979).
38. Annas, *The Rights of Hospital Patients*, 112–18 (1975).
39. *Id.* at 137–38; H. Pilpel, *Minors' Rights to Medical Care*, 36 Alb. L. Rev. 462, 472–87 (1972).
40. Bellotti v. Baird, 443 U.S. 622 (1979); Doe v. Irwin, 441 F. Supp. 1247 (W.D. Mich. 1977).

VIII

Advance Directives and Living Wills

Many persons would like to be sure that they do not receive excessive or burdensome treatments that merely prolong dying or life in a severely damaged state. Some court decisions suggest that directives for stopping treatment made while the person is competent, could be legally followed when the person becomes incompetent. Since 1976, twelve states have passed legislation authorizing such directives, and they have been recognized judicially by one state. Advance directives for medical care, sometimes called living wills, are an important device for permitting people to determine the medical care they will receive during critical illness. This chapter discusses the legal rights and duties that surround advance directives for medical care.

What is a living will?

A living will is a written directive to the family, physicians, and other health-care providers, made while a person is competent, to stop medical care if she becomes incompetent, and thus unable to express her wishes about stopping treatment. A legally binding living will accomplishes this purpose in two ways. First, it gives the doctor who relies on the directive immunity from civil and criminal liability for withholding care. Second, it requires that the doctor either follow the directives for withholding care, or remove herself from the case. It is called a "living will" because it controls events at a later time when the patient is still alive, but incompetent, in contrast to wills devising property which control events upon a person's death.

Why should a person make a living will?

A person should make a living will if he is concerned about receiving excessive, burdensome, or merely life-prolonging medical treatments when he is critically ill and not able to state his preferences. The living will provides a way for the person to refuse such treatment in advance. Doctors and families will have a firmer basis for stopping such treatments if the person has previously opposed them. (A prior directive in favor of treatment may also assure that some treatments that might otherwise be withheld, are provided.)

However, a person should not make a living will if he is unsure about the medical treatments he would want if he became incompetent, or if he thinks that once in the projected situation, he would choose differently than he thought he would in advance.

Does a person have a right to make a living will?

It depends. Any adult may give an oral or written directive to her doctor and family stating how she would like to be treated if she became incompetent and need medical care. However, whether the directive is binding on doctors or has any legal effect, depends on state law at the time that the need for treatment arises.

What states have passed living will laws?

Alabama, Arkansas, California, Idaho, Kansas, Nevada, New Mexico, North Carolina, Oregon, Texas, Vermont, Washington, and the District of Columbia have passed legislation authorizing living wills in various circumstances.[1] (Many other states have considered legislation, and some are likely to enact them in the future.)[2] Living will laws have different names. Most are called natural death, death with dignity, or right to die laws, and usually do not use the term *living will*. They all, however, try to preserve self-determination in medical care, by giving legal effect to advance directives for stopping treatment when a person is no longer able to decide.

Although these laws make living wills legally binding only if the person is terminally ill, they usually state that they are cumulative and do not restrict or impair any existing legal rights to have treatment withheld.[3] Thus, living wills may also be given effect in situations other than those specified in the legislation, depending on preexisting state law for stopping treatment by advance directive.

Are living wills legally binding in states that have not passed living will legislation?

Yes. Living wills may also be legally binding in states without living will legislation. With the exception of New York, the courts have not yet specifically decided whether a competent person has the right to issue binding directives regarding the medical care he receives when incompetent. But there are strong reasons for thinking that the courts would find them legally binding. Ordinarily, a doctor may treat a patient only if the patient has freely entered into the doctor-patient relationship and consented to treatment. It could be argued that an advance directive withdraws consent to certain treatments when the patient is incompetent to decide, since the directive asks that such treatment be withheld.

A constitutional basis for giving effect to patient directives for treatment when incompetent, was recently developed in the *Quinlan*[4] and *Saikewicz*[5] cases discussed in chapter V. Those cases specifically held that an incompetent patient retains a right of privacy to refuse medical treatment, which can be exercised by a court or guardian on the incompetent's behalf. The proxy for the incompetent is to ascertain what the patient would want if aware of her situation and able to voice her preferences. Though those cases did not involve a living will, they strongly imply that a competent person's directive regarding medical care when incompetent, might be found legally binding without specific legislation. Similarly, courts will often honor religious objections to medical treatment even when the person becomes incompetent and is no longer able to assert them.[6]

The 1981 New York case of *Eichner* v. *Dillon*[7] allows doctors to rely on prior directives in terminating treatment on incompetent patients. An eighty-year-old priest was irreversibly comatose, due to brain damage suffered after a cardiac arrest during a hernia operation. There was unchallenged evidence that in 1976, when the *Quinlan* case arose, and on later occasions, the patient had expressed his views about the case. He had stated that he agreed with the Roman Catholic position that the respirator in the *Quinlan* case was an "extraordinary treatment," and that "he would not want any of this 'extraordinary business' done for him under those circumstances."[8] Only a couple of months before the operation, he again stated that he would "not want his life prolonged by such measures if his condition were hopeless."[8A] On the basis of this evidence, the New York Court of Appeals ruled that the patient's prior expressed wish could be followed and the respirator could be turned off.

The *Eichner* decision does leave unanswered many questions that living will legislation specifically answers. However, it squarely supports the proposition that in the absence of legislation, physicians who rely on living wills to stop treatment, are acting reasonably and legally. A written living will (see p. 168), will probably meet the clear and convincing standard of proof that the patient had actually expressed such a wish. In addition, as the facts of *Eichner* itself shows, an oral discussion with friends or physicians could meet this standard as well. *Eichner* thus gives legal effect to most prior directives even without legislation. Since other courts are likely to follow this position, persons in states without living will laws should not wait for legislation to pass to begin using them.

May a doctor rely on a living will to stop treatment in states that have not passed living will laws?
It depends. Many persons in states without living will laws have made living wills with the hope that their families and doctors will follow them. While doctors sometimes follow them, other doctors disagree with the choice or are concerned that by stopping treatment, civil or criminal liability charges could be levied against them. To be on the safe side, they continue treatment until there is a clearer indication that it is no longer legally required.

In states without living will laws there are two situations in which a doctor may safely follow a living will, and a third where he should not. The first two involve situations where regardless of a living will, the doctor could legally withhold such care on the theory that the patient, if able to choose, would decide against treatment. In such cases, a living will does not create a right or duty that would not otherwise exist. But it does increase the possibility that the patient's existing right not to be treated will be observed, for it might clarify the doctor's legal duty, and remind him that he may stop treatments not in the patient's interest.

The second situation in which a doctor could safely "rely" on the living will, is when it is difficult to tell whether treatment is legally required because it is not clear if such treatment is in the patient's interest. In ambiguous situations the doctor who relies on a living will to define the patient's interests, does not violate the patient's rights and would not be subject to liability. However, the doctor must have reasonable grounds for thinking that the directive had been freely made and not revoked. A doctor who relied on a living will that had been made in his presence, or that had been witnessed and notarized and then presented to the doctor when the patient was competent, would be acting reasonably. If the matter had never been discussed, and a relative comes forward with a living will said to have been made by the patient, the doctor should take steps to assure that it was validly made. If the doctor acts reasonably and in good faith in his determination, reliance on a living will as evidence of the patient's interests will not lead to liability.

The situation where a doctor should not rely on a living will absent legislation is where treatment clearly appears to be in the patient's interests, and hence legally required, but a living will directs that it be withheld. The doctor who followed such directive without legislative or judicial authority, would take the risk that the courts would find that a competent patient may not, without legislation, control in advance, the care that he receives when incompetent; thus the doctor could be civilly or criminally liable for prematurely causing the patient's death. A more preferable course of action would be to ask the courts to decide whether the patient's prior wishes have priority. Resort to the courts would protect the doctor against liability, assure that the patient's rights are protected, and possibly bring about a judicial decision on the legal effect of living wills in states without legislation.

May a doctor ignore a living will in a state that has not passed a living will law?

It depends. In the situation where treatment would not be legally required because it offers the patient little benefit and great burdens, and would thus violate his right, the doctor would have an obligation not to treat, whether or not a living will so directs.

On the other hand, if treatment were in the incompetent patient's interest, but the patient had refused in advance through a living will, the doctor may be legally obligated to follow the patient's prior directive. The doctor's right to ignore the living will in such circumstances would depend upon whether the courts of the state involved would recognize the competent patient's right to issue binding directives concerning medical treatment when incompetent, a question that has not yet been definitively settled. A doctor aware of a living will that appeared to have been freely made, could not necessarily assume that treatment was in the patient's interest and therefore required, even if the guardian or family thought it was. The doctor's overriding duty is to his patient. If there is doubt about the patient's interest, he should seek a judicial ruling on whether the patient's current interests or the prior directive control. Otherwise, a decision to ignore the prior directive may violate the patient's right not to be treated. The doctor could be sued for battery, intentional infliction of emotional harm, or the cost of the additional care. However, a suit in such a situation is highly unlikely, especially when the family has insisted on treatment.

In states with living will laws, may a person direct that treatment be withheld in situations other than terminal illness?

Probably, but not according to the terms of the living will statutes. Those laws generally authorize competent patients to make legally binding directives against medical treatment when they are incompetent and are terminally ill.[9] Because the impetus for these laws was the plight of the terminally ill whose dying was unnecessarily prolonged, the laws do not by their terms authorize advance directives in situations where patients are comatose, chronically vegetative, mentally or physically disabled, or would object to certain treatments on religious grounds.

However, the restriction of current living will laws to terminal illness does not mean that directives to stop treatment in nonterminal situations would not be legally binding. Living will laws usually state that they "do not impair or supercede any legal right or responsibility which any person may have to effect the withholding or withdrawal of life-sustaining procedures in any lawful manner."[10] Whether a nonterminal directive will be legally binding thus depends on whether state law, independently of the living will law, would give legal effect to such a directive. If the patient's situation was such that treatment would not benefit the patient (and hence not be legally required), reliance on a nonterminal directive is not likely to lead to liability for abandoning or causing the death of the patient. (If the family disagreed, however, the doctor should ask a court to decide the matter). A nonterminal directive could also clarify whether treatment is in the patient's interest in situations of ambiguity, or where reasonable people might differ over what serves a person's interests.

The question is trickier when treatment would otherwise seem to be in the patient's interest, yet the directive orders that it be stopped, such as rejecting blood transfusions that would enable the patient to live a healthy life. There is a strong legal argument that such directives are binding because they are the best way for the incompetent person to exercise her constitutional right of privacy to refuse necessary treatment. However, until there is specific legislation or court decisions, doctors faced with nonterminal directives objecting to treatment that would otherwise be in the patient's interest, should seek advance judicial approval for stopping treatment. It is likely that courts will recognize the validity of the directive, particularly in states that follow *Quinlan, Saikewicz,* and *Eichner*. Then nonterminal directives would be legally binding in states with living will laws restricted to terminal conditions.

In states with living will legislation, may doctors stop treatment, relying on the provisions of the living will?

Yes. If the situation specified in the will and authorized by the statute has come about, and the doctor has reason to think that the directive is valid, she may rely on the living will and stop life-prolonging treatment without civil or criminal liability. The existence of the signed directive, witnessed and dated as required by the statute, may be taken as evidence of the patient's wishes in the situation. However, for a living will to be binding, some statutes require that two doctors agree that the patient has "an incurable injury, disease or illness certified to be a terminal condition,"[11] and that "death will occur whether or not life-sustaining procedures are utilized and where the application of life-sustaining measures would serve only to prolong the dying process."[12] Some also require that the doctors find that "death is imminent, whether or not life-sustaining procedures are used."[13]

In states with living will legislation, may a doctor refuse to follow a directive in a living will to stop treatment?

No. The doctor is obligated to follow the patient's directive if the situation in the directive and authorized by the statute, has come about. The doctor who refuses to follow the living will must transfer the patient to another doctor, or be subject to discipline by the state medical examining board for unprofessional conduct.[14] She could also be sued for breach of contract, battery, intentional infliction of harm to the patient and family, forfeit her right to fees for medical services provided contrary to the directive, and be liable for any additional medical expenses. However, if the doctor has reasonable grounds for thinking that the will was not a free or accurate expression of the patient's wishes, she could probably legally refuse to follow it.

In California and states that follow the California model (Alabama, District of Columbia, Oregon and Texas), the doctor must follow the directive only if the patient is a "qualified person." A person is "qualified" if he "signed a directive 14 days after two physicians have diagnosed and certified in writing that he/she is afflicted with a terminal illness or injury."[15] If the patient is not a "qualified person," or the living will specifies situations not authorized by the statute, the doctor's obligation to follow the will, will depend on the patient's preexisting right under state law to refuse treatment in advance (see p. 102).

A patient can avoid the possibility that a doctor will not follow his directive, by giving a copy to the doctor and discussing it with him. He should ask the doctor to agree to follow the directive, whether or not he is legally bound to, and ask the doctor to sign a statement in the will, acknowledging it and agreeing to honor it. A doctor who failed to honor the will could then be sued for breach of contract, as well as for lack of consent to treatment, and be ordered by a court to terminate treatment.

If the doctor refuses to comply with the patient's directions for nontreatment, family and friends seeking to protect the rights of the patients should try to have the patient transferred to the care of another doctor. If that cannot be arranged, they should ask the courts to order that the will be followed. Or, they may also sue the doctor for damages for wrongful treatment and for any medical bills incurred as a result.

Are there any restrictions on the kinds of treatment that a person can order withheld by a living will?

No. The purpose of the living will is to enable the patient to exercise his constitutional right to refuse medical treatment before he becomes incompetent to do so. This would include a wide range of treatments, including those that can cure the patient, as well as those that will merely postpone the moment of death. Living will laws, however, are vague about the treatments that the patient in advance can order stopped, using such nonspecific terms as "life-sustaining," "extraordinary means," and "artificial means." The intent of living will laws is to enable the patient to refuse treatment that does not cure or rehabilitate, but merely maintains bodily processes or prolongs dying. The person making the living will, to avoid problems of interpretation, could list specific medical procedures that she wants withheld. In addition to general descriptions by activity, purpose, or outcome, these might include respirators, heart massage, pacemakers, defibrillators, kidney machines, organ transplantation, blood transfusions, surgery, intubation, medications such as antibiotics or vasopressors, and nasogastric or intravenous feeding. The directive might clearly state that the patient wants treatment to relieve pain, even if other essential treatments are stopped.

Must a living will follow any particular form to be valid?

It depends on the state. Some states[16] set forth a document that must be followed precisely for a living will to be valid. Other states[17] suggest a form but allow a variation in terminology.

In states without living will laws, it's more likely that the living will would be followed by doctors, families, and the courts, if it appeared informed, complete, and voluntary. Following one of the statutory forms, or the ones that have been recommended by such organizations as the Society for the Right to Die, and Concern for Dying, would more likely be given effect, especially if it has been witnessed and notarized. Three representative forms are included in the Appendix.

Must a living will be witnessed to be valid?

Not necessarily. Living will statutes generally require that the directive be signed and dated in the presence of two witnesses. A few states also require that the directive be notarized, signed in court, or filed with a court clerk.[18] Living wills that do not strictly comply with the witness provisions might still be considered legal, but doctors would be less likely to rely on them.

The witness requirement serves the useful purpose of protecting the signer of the will from fraud, undue influence, and impulsive choice. Also, doctors and families are more likely to honor a witnessed directive, because it lessens doubt about its validity.

Most living will laws place some limitations on who may serve as a witness. For example, in California, witnesses may not be (1) related to the declarant by blood or marriage; (2) entitled to any portion of the declarant's estate; or (3) employed by the attending physician or patient's health facility.[19] California also requires that one of the two witnesses for nursing home patients be a patient advocate.[20] These provisions might exclude as witnesses, almost all persons to whom a patient has ready access, or who may need to be aware of the directive if it is to be followed. Arkansas and New Mexico, on the other hand, place no limit on who may be a witness.[21]

In states without living will laws there is no witness requirement as such. However, there would be fewer doubts raised, and fewer refusals to accept the will as valid, if it is witnessed. Lawyers drafting living wills in those states should follow state probate code provisions for making property wills, which usually require two witnesses.

How long is a living will valid? Must it be reexecuted?

A living will is generally effective from the moment it is made, unless the signer specifies otherwise. If the maker becomes incompetent immediately after signing and the situation described in the will occurs, the living will could be relied on by doctors in withholding care, and they could be obligated to follow it. In California, however, doctors have the option of not following the directive unless it has been executed fourteen days after two doctors have certified in writing, that the patient has a terminal condition.[22] New Mexico, Nevada, Arkansas, North Carolina, and states without living will laws, place no time limit on the validity of the living will.[23]

Alabama, California, District of Columbia, Oregon, Texas, Vermont, and Idaho, on the other hand, require that the directive be reexecuted every five years.[24] While periodic renewal requirements may assure that the living will represents the person's current wishes, they should not apply to persons who become physically or mentally incapable of reexecution.

Can a person change his mind and revoke a living will?
Yes. At any time. The will reflects the person's wishes, while competent, of how he would like to be treated if certain situations of incompetency and medical need arise. If the person changes his mind, he is free to revoke the will, even if there is doubt about his competency. Revocation means that the patient, when incompetent, will be treated as the law would otherwise require, rather than as the will directs.

A person can revoke a living will by burning, tearing, canceling, or obliterating the document, or by signing a witnessed and notarized statement that it is revoked. Most statutes also allow oral revocation, although this may not be binding on a doctor if he has not received actual notice of the revocation.[25] A person who wishes to revoke a living will should inform his physician, family, or closest friends, and have a written revocation placed in his medical record.

Can one person revoke a living will for another person?
Not unless the person is acting at the direction of the signer of the will and the direction is competently and freely given. Such a person may then revoke the living will by manually destroying or obliterating it or by informing the doctor and the family of the person's intent to revoke the will.[26] A doctor so informed is then obligated to honor the revocation, and treat, unless she has reason to think that it was not freely and competently made. In that case, she should seek a judicial ruling on the legality of withholding care on the basis of the living will that she has been told the patient intended to revoke. Otherwise, she could be civilly or criminally liable for unreasonably relying on an invalid living will.

May a person be denied admission to a hospital or a health insurance policy because she has not signed a living will?
Probably not. Most states with living will laws specifically prohibit health care providers or insurers, from conditioning

treatment on the existence of a living will.[27] States without such laws are likely to maintain that living wills drawn up in order to qualify for health services or insurance, are invalid because made under duress, or are against public policy.[28] In fact, forcing a person to make a living will that she would not otherwise make, which leads to an earlier death than would have occurred because treatment in the patient's interests would then be withheld, would violate the patient's rights, and could lead to criminal and civil penalties.

Does the refusal of medical treatment through a living will, constitute suicide?

No. Most living will laws explicitly state that a patient's death caused by the withholding or withdrawal of life-sustaining procedures in accordance with a living will, is not suicide.[29] Most laws also state that a living will will not effect the benefits paid under life insurance policies.[30] In the three states with living will laws that have not addressed the issue,[31] it is unlikely that such deaths would be considered suicide, since the purpose of the laws is to recognize the individual's right to refuse necessary medical treatments that could prolong life. In states without living will laws, death caused by the withdrawal of care pursuant to a living will, is not likely to be considered suicide since a competent patient's refusal of treatment in those circumstances would not be considered suicide.[32]

Is a lawyer necessary to make a living will?

No. Any person may write and sign a document directing that medical care be stopped when incompetent, without first consulting a lawyer. Forms to follow are readily available (see the Appendix).

However, a lawyer could be helpful in several ways. He could inform a person of the requirements, if any, under state living will laws; advise him about the form to be followed in states without laws; explain the legal significance of various terms and provisions; clarify the choices and decisions that a person must face in making a living will; and suggest language or provisions that will make compliance with the living will more likely.

Where should a person keep a living will?

In a safe place that will provide easy access for those whose actions are affected by the living will. He should also give copies of it to his family and doctor. The patient should ask that it be placed or noted in his medical record, and may also want to carry a small card on his person that states that a living will exists in a certain place, and summarizes its content.

May a person specify in a living will that he wants all possible treatment, no matter what the cost?
Yes. A living will is a directive regarding the medical care the person would like to receive if he becomes incompetent. Although its primary purpose is to enable a person not to be treated in certain situations of incompetency, there is no reason why it could not also direct how a person is to be treated. Such a directive would be useful in situations where the person's interests are unclear, and it would remind physicians and the family of the incompetent person's right to be treated.

None of the current living will laws, with the exception of Arkansas,[33] address this issue. The legal effect of such a directive would depend on legal requirements for treatment of incompetents, and the extent to which state law would recognize a competent person's directive. Ordinarily, an incompetent patient would have a right to medical treatment as long as the benefits of treatment outweigh the burdens, and a directive that he wishes to be treated would not be necessary. However, if a person is fearful that doctors will mistakenly withhold treatment, requesting treatment in a living will may assure that treatment occurs. Also, a suit to protect the patient's right to be treated would be strengthened if an explicit directive for treatment had been violated.

On the other hand, if treatment is not clearly in the patient's interest, there would be no legal duty to provide it. The benefit to an incompetent patient may be independent of any prior directive. An incompetent person who faces imminent death may gain little from repeated cardiopulmonary resuscitation, even if there were a prior directive instructing that such treatment be provided. Similarly, there is no legal duty to treat a person who was irreversibly comatose, even though a living will had directed that "extraordinary means be utilized to prolong life."

May a person direct in a living will that he be actively killed if he will linger on in great suffering if withdrawal of treatment occurs?

No. Since prior consent is no defense for homicide, a competent person has no legal right to insist on active euthanasia, even if he is in great suffering and cannot cause his own death.[34] Unfortunately, the effect of such a policy would be that persons who have asked that all treatment be stopped might linger on in a painful, incapacitated state for some time. Usually, however, their pain can be alleviated with drugs, and if they are terminal or severely ill, will probably not linger long.

How can a person be sure that his living will will be followed?

First, he should follow the applicable statute in a state with a living will law, so that all requirements are met. In states without legislation, a lawyer should be consulted and a living will should be drawn up that follows the form of an applicable state law or the state probate code. At least two persons should witness it and it should be notarized.

Second, the person should inform his immediate family and doctor of his decision and give them copies of the living will. He should ask his doctor to agree to abide by it, and have him sign it. If the doctor refuses, the person should seek a doctor who will agree to follow the directive when he becomes incompetent. He should also ask that a copy be placed in his medical record, and that nurses and others caring for him, be informed of the directive when he is admitted to the hospital.

Third, he should reexecute the directive every five years, to make sure that it reflects his current thinking, whether or not this is required by state law.

Finally, the person should enlist a close relative or friend to act as his advocate and assure compliance with the living will when he enters the hospital. Such a person could be named in the living will as the patient's agent for all decisions about his medical treatment, if he becomes incompetent, though such an appointment may not be legally binding.

What if a person destroys or revokes a person's living will without his consent?

Most living will statutes make such action a misdemeanor.[35] Such a person could also be sued by the patient or his

estate for the pain, suffering, and expense caused by unwanted or excessive treatment that the living will would have
prevented.

**What if a person forges a living will, or conceals its
revocation so that the person dies sooner than they otherwise would?**

A person who intentionally forges another's signature to a
living will, or conceals or withholds knowledge of a revocation, has, if his actions lead to terminating treatment that
would otherwise have been in the patient's interest, caused
the patient's death. Most states would treat this as some form
of homicide, with some living will laws making it a separate
felony.[36] In addition, the person could be sued civilly for
wrongful death of the patient.

**May a person appoint, in a living will, another person to
make treatment decisions while she is incompetent?**

None of the current living will laws authorize a competent
person to invest another person with legal power to make
treatment decisions for him when he is incompetent. However, many states have "durable" power of attorney statutes,
which authorize a person to appoint another agent to make
his decisions when he becomes incompetent.[37] (At common
law, a power of attorney ended with the incompetency or
death of the appointer).[38] The terms of many of these statutes is broad enough to cover the appointment of agents for
medical care decisions that arise when the patient becomes
incompetent.[39] However, no case has yet dealt with this
issue, and doctors and families are not likely to follow the
orders of such an agent without specific legislative or judicial
authority for doing so. A bill giving a person the power to
appoint an agent for medical treatment decisions during incompetency has been introduced in Michigan.

Pending such legislation, persons may still make written
directives appointing another person their agent for medical
treatment decisions when they are incompetent, but there is
no guarantee that doctors and families would follow their
recommendations. Unless a court has appointed that person
the patient's guardian, doctors would not be legally required
to follow the designated agent's perception of the patient's
best interest, though the agent might help in deciding what is
in a patient's interests. A doctor who relied on the agent's

advice to make decisions in ambiguous situations, would probably be acting reasonably. However, an agent's claim that the patient would want treatment withheld when it would otherwise appear in the patient's interest to be treated, should not be automatically followed. In that case, the doctor should seek the appointment of a guardian to determine care, or otherwise have the patient's rights clarified. The court might make the designated agent the guardian. In any event, the agent's knowledge of the patient and his previously expressed wishes, would be relevant in determining the patient's interests in further treatment.

NOTES

1. Ala. Acts 1981, No. 81–772, p. 1329; ARK. STAT. ANN. §§ 82–3801 to 82–3804 (Supp. 1979); CAL. HEALTH & SAFETY CODE §§ 7185 to 7195 (West Supp. 1980); D.C. Code, Title 6, ch. 24 (Sub. II, 1981 Ed.); IDA. CODE §§ 39–4501 to 39–4508 (Supp. 1980); KAN. STAT. ANN. §§ 65–28, 101 to 65–28, 190 (Supp. 1979); NEV. REV. STAT. §§ 449, 540 to 449.690 (1979); N.M. STAT. ANN. §§ 24–7–1 to 24–7–11 (1978); N.C. GEN. STAT. §§ 90–320 to 90–321 (Supp. 1979); ORE. REV. STAT. §§ 97.050 to 97.090 (1979); TEX. REV. CIV. STAT. ANN. art. 4590h (Vernon Supp. 1980); 18 Vt. Stat. Ann. § 111 (1982); WASH. REV. CODE ANN. §§ 70.122.010 to 70.122.905 (Supp. 1980).
2. Note, *Rejection of Extraordinary Medical Care By a Terminal Patient: A Proposed Living Will Statute*, 64 Iowa L. Rev. 573 (1979).
3. CAL. HEALTH & SAFETY CODE §§ 7193 (West Supp. 1980); IDA. CODE § 39–4508 (Supp. 1980); KAN. STAT. ANN. § 65–28, 108(d) (Supp. 1979); NEV. REV. STAT. § 449.680 (1979); N.M. STAT. ANN. § 24–7–9 (1978); N.C. GEN. STAT. § 90–320(b) (Supp. 1979); ORE. REV. STAT. § 97.085(2) (1979); TEX. REV. CIV. STAT. ANN. art. 4590h § 11 (Vernon Supp. 1980).
4. Matter of Quinlan, 70 N.J. 10, 355 A.2d 647 (1975).
5. 373 Mass. 728, 370 N.E. 2d 417 (1977).
6. Winters v. Miller, 446 F.2d 65 (2nd Cir. 1971); *In re* Lucille Boyd, 403 A.2d 744 (1979).
7. 420 N.E. 2d 64 (1981);
8. *Id*. at 406.
8A. *Id*. See also p. 410.
9. See, e.g., CAL. HEALTH & SAFETY CODE § 7188 (West Supp. 1980); KAN. STAT. ANN. § 65–28, 103 (Supp. 1979); TEX. REV. CIV. STAT. ANN. art. 4590h § 3 (Vernon Supp. 1980).
10. CAL. HEALTH & SAFETY CODE § 7193 (West Supp. 1980); IDA. CODE § 39–4508 (Supp. 1980); KAN. STAT. ANN. § 65–28, 108(d) (Supp. 1979); NEV. REV. STAT. § 449.680 (1979); N.M. STAT. ANN. § 24–7–9

(1978); N.C. GEN. STAT. § 90–320(b) (Supp. 1979); ORE. REV. STAT. § 97.085(2) (1979); TEX. REV. CIV. STAT. ANN. art. 4590h § 11 (Vernon Supp. 1980).

11. CAL. HEALTH & SAFETY CODE § 7188 (West Supp. 1980); KAN. STAT. ANN. § 65–28, 103 (Supp. 1979); ORE. REV. STAT. § 97.055 (1979); WASH. REV. CODE ANN. § 70.122.030 (Supp. 1980).

12. KAN. STAT. ANN. § 65–28, 103; WASH. REV. CODE ANN. § 70.122.030.

13. CAL. HEALTH & SAFETY CODE § 7188 (West Supp. 1980); IDA. CODE § 39–4504 (Supp. 1980); ORE. REV. STAT. § 97.055 (1979); TEX. REV. CIV. STAT. ANN. art. 4590h § 3 (Vernon Supp. 1980); WASH. REV. CODE ANN. § 70.122.030 (Supp. 1980).

14. CAL. HEALTH & SAFETY CODE § 7191(b) (West Supp. 1980).

15. CAL. HEALTH & SAFETY CODE §§ 7187(e) and 7191(b) (West Supp. 1980).

16. CAL. HEALTH & SAFETY CODE § 7188 (West Supp. 1980); IDA. CODE § 39–4504 (Supp. 1980); ORE. REV. STAT. § 97.055 (1979); TEX. REV. CIV. STAT. ANN. art. 4590h § 3 (Vernon Supp. 1980).

17. KAN. STAT. ANN. § 65–28, 103 (Supp. 1979). NEV. REV. STAT. § 449.610 (1979); N.C. GEN. STAT. § 90–321 (1979); WASH. REV. CODE ANN. § 70.122.030 (Supp. 1980).

18. IDA. CODE § 39–4504 (Supp. 1980); N.C. GEN. STAT. § 90–321 (1979); TEX. REV. CIV. STAT. ANN. art. 4590h § 3 (Vernon Supp. 1980).

19. CAL. HEALTH & SAFETY CODE § 7188 (West Supp. 1980).

20. CAL. HEALTH & SAFETY CODE § 7188.5 (West Supp. 1980).

21. ARK. STAT. ANN. § 82–3802 (Supp. 1979); N.M. STAT. ANN. § 24–7–3 (1978).

22. CAL. HEALTH & SAFETY CODE § 7191(c) (West Supp. 1980).

23. N.M. STAT. ANN. § 24–7–3 (1978); NEV. REV. STAT. § 449.610 (1979); ARK. STAT. ANN. § 82–3802 (Supp. 1979); N.C. GEN. STAT. § 90–321(i) (Supp. 1979).

24. Ala. Acts 1981, No. 81–772, p.1329; CAL. HEALTH & SAFETY CODE § 7189.5 (West Supp. 1980); D.C. Code, Title 6, ch. 24 (Sub. II, 1981 Ed.); ORE. REV. STAT. § 97.055(6) (1979); IDA. CODE § 39–4506 (Supp. 1980).

25. CAL. HEALTH & SAFETY CODE § 7189(b) (West Supp. 1980); IDA. CODE § 39–4505(2) (Supp. 1980); KAN. STAT. ANN. § 65–28, 104(b) (Supp. 1979); NEV. REV. STAT. § 449.620(2) (1979); N.M. STAT. ANN. § 24–7–7–(A) (1978); ORE. REV. STAT. § 97.065(3) (1979); TEX. REV. CIV. ANN. art. 4590h § 4(b) (Vernon Supp. 1980); WASH. REV. CODE ANN. § 70.122.040(2) (Supp. 1980).

26. CAL. HEALTH & SAFETY CODE § 7189 (West Supp. 1980); IDA. CODE § 39–4505 (Supp. 1980); KAN. STAT. ANN. § 65–28, 104 (Supp. 1979); NEV. REV. STAT. § 449.620 (1979); N.M. STAT. ANN. § 24–7–7(A) (1978); ORE. REV. STAT. § 97.065(3) (1979); TEX. REV. CIV. STAT. ANN. art. 4590h § 4(b) (Vernon Supp. 1980); WASH. REV. CODE ANN. § 70.122.040 (Supp. 1980).

27. CAL. HEALTH & SAFETY CODE § 7192(c) (West Supp. 1980); IDA. CODE § 39–4508(3) (Supp. 1980); KAN. STAT. ANN. § 65–28, 108(c) (Supp. 1979); NEV. REV. STAT. § 449.650(3) (1979); N.M. STAT. ANN. § 24–7–8 (1978); N.C. GEN. STAT. § 90–321(g) (Supp. 1979); ORE. REV. STAT. § 97.080(2) (1979); TEX. REV. CIV. STAT. ANN. art. 4590h § 8(c) (Vernon Supp. 1980); WASH. REV. CODE ANN § 70.122.070(3) (Supp. 1980).

28. The legal analysis of this problem is likely to follow the analysis for hospital-imposed releases, Tunkl v. Regents of University of California, 60 Cal. 2d 92, 32 Cal. Rptr. 33, 383 P.2d 441, and for agreements to arbitrate, Wheeler v. St. Joseph Hospital, 133 Cal. Rptr. 775. On the latter issue, see generally Henderson, *Contractual Problems in the Enforcement of Agreements to Arbitrate Medical Malpractice*, 58 Va. L. Rev. 947 (1972).

29. CAL. HEALTH & SAFETY CODE § 7192(a) (West Supp. 1980); KAN. STAT. ANN. § 65–28, 108(a) (Supp. 1979); NEV. REV. STAT. § 449.650(1) (1979); N.M. STAT. ANN. § 24–7–8 (1978); N.C. GEN. STAT. § 90–321(f) (Supp. 1979); ORE. REV. STAT. § 97.085(3) (1979); TEX. REV. CIV. STAT. ANN. art. 4590h § 8(a) (Vernon Supp. 1980); WASH. REV. CODE ANN. § 70.122.070(1) (Supp. 1980).

30. CAL. HEALTH & SAFETY CODE § 7192(b) (West Supp. 1980); IDA. CODE § 3904508(2) (Supp. 1980); KAN. STAT. ANN. § 65–28, 108(b) (Supp. 1979); NEV. REV. STAT. § 449.650(2) (1979); N.M. STAT. ANN. § 24–7–8(B); ORE. REV. STAT. § 97.080(3) (1979); TEX. REV. CIV. STAT. ANN. art. 4590h § 8(b); (Vernon Supp. 1980); WASH. REV. CODE ANN. § 70.122.070(2) (Supp. 1980).

31. ARK. STAT. ANN. §§ 82–3801 to 82–3804 (Supp. 1979); IDA. CODE §§ 39–4501 to 39–4508 (Supp. 1980).

32. See chapter I, p. 5; Note, *Suicide and the Compulsion of Life Saving Medical Procedures: An Analysis of the Refusal of Treatment Cases*, 44 Bklyn. L. Rev. 285 (1978).

33. ARK STAT. ANN. § 82–3802 (Supp. 1979).

34. See chapter I, p. 5.

35. CAL. HEALTH & SAFETY CODE § 7194 (West Supp. 1980); KAN. STAT. ANN. § 65–28, 107(b) (Supp. 1979); NEV. REV. STAT. § 449.660(1) (1979); TEX. REV. CIV. STAT. ANN. art. 4590h § 9 (Vernon Supp. 1980); WASH. REV. CODE ANN. § 70.122.090 (Supp. 1980).

36. Homicide: CAL. HEALTH & SAFETY CODE § 7194 (West Supp. 1980); NEV. REV. STAT. § 449.660(2) (1979); TEX. REV. CIV. STAT. ANN. art. 4590h § 9 (Vernon Supp. 1980); WASH. REV. CODE ANN. § 70.122.090 (Supp. 1980).

37. CONN. GEN. STAT. § 45–690 (1980); FLA. STAT. ANN. § 709.08 (West 1980); IDA. CODE § 15–5–501 (1979); MICH. COMP. LAWS ANN. § 700.495 (1980); PA. STAT. ANN. tit. 20, § 5601 (Purdon 1975); UTAH CODE ANN. § 75–5–501 (1978).

38. 24 Corpus Juris Secondum, Agency, § 135–141 (1972); Restatement (Second) of Agency §§ 120–123 (1957).

39. See, e.g., Virginia Code § 11–9.1 to .2 (1950); Moses and Pope, *Estate Planning, Disability and the Durable Power of Attorney*, 30 S.C. L. Rev. 511 (1979). Karlsson, "Appointing an Agent for Medical Care Decisions under Durable Power of Attorney Statutes" (Aug. 1980). (Unpublished paper on file with author.)

40. Relman, *Michigan's Sensible 'Living Will,'* 300 N. Eng. J. Med. 1270–71 (1979).

IX

Brain Death

Traditionally, a person has been considered dead when his heart and lungs stopped functioning. Without oxygen carried by the blood, the organs of the body, including the brain, soon die. Advances in medical technology, however, have now made it possible to artificially maintain the functions of the heart and lungs indefinitely. These advances enable many patients to recover, but they also prolong heart and lung action in persons whose brains no longer function. The question arises as to whether these persons are dead.

The question is important for critically ill persons for at least two reasons. If patients are dead, they no longer need to be treated. Doctors could legally stop medical treatment at that point and families and friends could begin the grieving and other adjustments that accompany death. The second reason is to facilitate organ donations. If the person were dead before the artificially maintained circulation were stopped, the organs could be removed with a minimum of damage and a greater likelihood of successful transplantation.

Over the last fifteen years these concerns have led to a reconsideration of the criteria and tests by which death is determined, and medical and legal adoption of brain-related criteria of death. This chapter discusses the legal status of brain death, and its implications for the rights of critically ill patients.

What is brain death?
Brain death is the condition in which the brain completely and irreversibly loses all functions. When the brain is dead, all other organs of the body will also cease to function, unless

116

mechanical assistance enables them to survive. Since brain activity is essential for the attributes that make us persons, a person who has irreversible cessation of all brain activity, ceases to exist, even if the heart and lungs are artificially maintained. Thus, the death of the brain is equivalent to death itself, and criteria or signs that the brain has died, become criteria or signs that death has occurred.

Sometimes people confuse brain death, meaning the total destruction of brain function, with partial brain death, or destruction of certain parts of the brain, usually the cortex, in which the capacity for consciousness, communication, and interaction with others primarily resides. Although cerebral, or neocortical death, may indicate that all the brain has been destroyed, it is not considered a reliable indicator of total brain death because brain stem and other lower brain functions may continue, despite the loss of cortical activity. While some commentators have suggested that cortical brain death constitutes the death of the person, brain death ordinarily means total brain death, and will be so used here.

How is brain death determined?

Total brain death is determined by a series of medical tests. In the United States the tests generally used[2] concern patient response to stimuli, the presence of reflexes and spontaneous movements, and an electroencephalogram (EEG) which shows electrical activity in the brain. There must be no evidence of hypothermia, or subnormal body temperature, or drugs which depress brain function; these findings must persist over twenty-four hours.

These tests are often referred to as the "Harvard criteria," since they were first recommended in 1968 by an ad hoc committee of Harvard Medical School.[3] They are now widely accepted by the medical profession as reliable criteria that the brain has died. In fact, there is evidence that these criteria are too strict, and that total brain death can be reliably determined by clinical examination and tests in a period of as little as six hours.

Is brain death legally recognized?

Yes. Traditionally, the legal criterion for determining death was the total cessation of heart and lung activity. The common law defined death as "the cessation of life; the ceasing to exist; defined by physicians as a total stoppage of the circulation of the blood, and a cessation of the animal and vital functions consequent thereupon, such as respiration, pulse, etc."[4] When the lungs could no longer deliver oxygen to the body, the brain and other organs stopped functioning, and the body lost those characteristics essential to life.

Thirty-one states by legislation and several by court decision, have given legal recognition to brain-related criteria for death.[5] All thirty-one recognize that death may be pronounced on the basis of the irreversible cessation of brain function, and depend on medical judgment for determining brain death, since these are technical matters (and therefore should not be specified in legislation). A few statutes do, however, require that two physicians find a total loss of brain function before death can be pronounced on this basis,[6] and a few have other requirements.

The laws fit into four categories. One category follows the first brain death statute enacted in 1970 in Kansas[7] (Maryland, Virginia, New Mexico, Alaska, and Oregon) and allows the physician to determine death either by traditional heart and lung criteria, or by brain death criteria. It is important to emphasize that these alternate criteria do not suggest that there are two separate types of death; it means that there are two different ways of determining that death has occurred.

The second type of statute views death as a single phenomenon that can be determined by brain-related criteria only in situations where respiratory and circulatory functions are being maintained artificially[8] (Michigan, West Virginia, Georgia, Louisiana, Iowa, and Montana). It provides for one state or phenomenon, death, which can be determined by measuring its different manifestations. A typical statute of this type states:

> A person will be considered dead if in the announced opinion of a physician, based on ordinary standards of medical practice, he has experienced an irreversible cessation of spontaneous respiratory and circulatory functions. In the event that artificial means of support preclude a determination that these functions have ceased, a person will be considered dead if in the announced opinion of a physician based on ordinary practice, he has experienced an irreversible cessation of spontaneous brain functions. Death will have occurred at the time when the relevant functions ceased.[9]

A third category of law follows the suggestion of the Law and Medicine Committee of the American Bar Association, and simply states that "For all legal purposes, a human body with irreversible cessation of total brain function, according to usual and customary standards of medical practice, shall be considered dead"[10] (California, Georgia, Idaho, Illinois, Oklahoma, and Tennessee). Under this statute, a physician can determine that death has occurred based either on the cessation of heart and lung activity, which inevitably causes destruction of the brain, or by tests which specifically measure whether irreversible cessation of brain function has occurred.

A fourth kind of brain death statute is based on the Uniform Determination of Death Act. This model was developed in 1981 by the President's Commission for the Study of Ethical Problems in Medicine and Biomedical and Behavorial Research, in consultation with the American Bar Association, the American Medical Association and the National Conference of Commissioners on Uniform State Laws, in order to avoid the confusion and uncertainty arising from the different versions of brain death legislation. The Commission recommended that every state adopt the Uniform act, which states:

> An individual who has sustained either (1) irreversible cessation of circulatory and respiratory functions, or (2) irreversible cessation of all functions of the entire brain, including the brain stem, is dead. A determination of death must be made in accordance with medical standards.[11]

To date Colorado, Idaho, Mississippi, Vermont and Wisconsin have adopted this law.

Several states have also recognized the validity of brain-related criteria for death by judicial decision. The question arose in New York when doctors and hospitals sought a declaratory judgment to clarify, for purposes of organ transplantation, the terms *death*, and *time of death*, in the state's Anatomical Gift Act.[12] The court held that brain-related criteria of death were within the meaning of death as used in the statute, and urged the legislature to provide a statewide remedy for the problem. In Massachusetts, the question arose in the context of a murder trial.[13] The defendant had struck the deceased on the head with a baseball bat. When there was no longer any sign of brain activity, the doctors stopped the machines that were regulating his heart and lungs. The Massachusetts Supreme Judicial Court, like every other court faced with the issue in a criminal context,[14] rejected the defendant's argument that the doctors had killed the victim because the deceased was alive when they stopped the respirator. The court held that the person had died when his brain had lost all functioning, which had occurred before the respirator was turned off, and thus, the defendant, and not the doctors, was guilty of homicide. Courts in Minnesota,[15] Colorado,[16] and Washington,[17] have also granted legal validity to brain-related criteria of death in cases involving the termination of treatment on totally brain-dead patients.

Judicial recognition of brain-related criteria of death is usually an inadequate procedure for clarifying the rights and duties of doctors and patients in these situations. Usually the case will deal with only one consequence or aspect of death, such as criminal liability or organ donation, leaving physicians uncertain about what is legally required in other contexts. Although it's likely that the courts would extend brain-related criteria to these other contexts, a legislative solution would be more desirable. It would provide a uniform method of determining death for all purposes, help educate patients' families and the public about the meaning of brain death, and assure that physicians apply uniform criteria for determining death. The precise tests to be used do not have to be indicated in the statute, since these will change with medical knowledge and experience.

Is a brain-dead person legally dead in states without legislation or court decisions on brain death?

Probably. The courts in those states would probably grant legal validity to brain-related criteria of death if they were confronted with a case. Since every court that has faced this question has recognized brain death, it is highly unlikely that doctors who, on the basis of medically recognized tests, pronounced brain-dead people dead and acted accordingly, would be found liable, although a statute is desirable to reduce uncertainty.

May a doctor turn respirators off, and stop treatment on, patients who are brain dead?

Yes. Legally, a doctor may turn off a respirator on a brain-dead person. Disconnecting a respirator or stopping other treatment is not denying a brain-dead person anything that it is in his interest to have. The absence of an obligation to treat brain-dead persons would also exist in states that have not yet officially recognized brain death. When the question arises, the courts would probably rule that respirators may be turned off because such a person is legally dead. Alternatively, if the courts found that a person with no brain function was legally alive, they would probably still find that there was no duty to treat, since a brain-dead person would have no interest in receiving further treatment.[18]

Is the consent of the family or guardian of a brain-dead person necessary in order to have respirators and other treatment stopped?

No. Doctors may withhold further treatment without the family's consent without violating the patient's rights. To avoid misunderstanding, however, it might be advisable to consult the family.

There is one situation in which the consent of the family should be obtained before turning off a respirator. As next of kin, the family has a right over disposition of the deceased's body. If they want the body maintained for transplant or research purposes, the doctor may not legally stop respirators without their consent. If a dispute develops, a judicial ruling on the doctor's duty may be necessary.

Must doctors get court approval before they stop treatment on brain-dead persons?

No. When the person is brain dead, the doctor has no obligation to continue to treat him, and may even have a duty to stop treatment, unless the family orders otherwise. It is not legally necessary for him to get court approval. Indeed, maintaining brain-dead persons while seeking court approval, may cause great stress and suffering on the families and unnecessarily increase the deceased's hospital bills. Although a doctor may want to get advance judicial approval in a jurisdiction that has not yet officially recognized brain death, he runs little risk of liability in proceeding without court approval. Of course, if there is a dispute with the family, resort to the courts before turning off the respirator, will clarify the issue.

Is a doctor legally obligated to stop treatment on a brain-dead person?

Yes. Once the patient is known to be brain dead, the doctor has no further obligation to maintain him. Unless the family has consented to further maintenance of the brain-dead person, the doctor who maintains the body artificially, could be liable for desecration or mutilation, and for the costs of further treatment.

May doctors turn respirators off, and stop medical care on, people who are partially brain dead?

It depends. Persons who have lost some brain function, even the cerebral or cortical function that is associated with consciousness and the ability to interact with others, are not considered dead under any of the pertinent statutes or court decisions. Legally, only total brain death constitutes death.

The legality of turning off respirators on partially brain-dead persons thus depends on whether the benefits of continued treatment to such patients, outweigh the burdens, and thus would be chosen by the patient if she were competent.[19] If the patient's brain is so impaired that she is unconscious and unlikely to recover cognitive ability, treatment could be legally stopped. The *Quinlan*[20] and *Eichner*[21] cases have made it clear that there is no legal obligation to treat chronically vegetative patients.

May physicians turn respirators off on brain-dead patients if they have not repeated the necessary tests over a twenty-four hour period?

It depends. The Harvard criteria for brain death have been widely adopted by the medical profession and thus constitute the "ordinary standards of medical practice" for determining the "irreversible cessation of spontaneous brain function" required by the statutes and cases recognizing brain death. Unless medical practice changes significantly, or a substantial minority of doctors determine brain death by less restrictive criteria, a doctor who pronounced a person dead and stopped a respirator on the basis of tests less certain than the Harvard criteria, would be departing from ordinary standards of medical practice.

While such a practice is neither medically nor legally advisable, and is more likely to lead to suits, it is not necessarily illegal, though if it violates hospital policy, hospital privileges could be restricted. It would lead to civil or criminal liability only if in fact there was evidence that the person (1) was not brain dead, and (2) it was in his interest to be kept on the respirator. Failing to follow the standard tests for brain death does not necessarily prove either (1) or (2). The person could still have been brain dead, despite the failure to use the standard tests. Even if he were not, he still might not fall into that category of incompetent patients who must legally be treated because treatment is in their interests. Liability would thus depend on how likely it was, in light of the tests that were done and other evidence, that the person was alive and had a right to be treated.

Can a brain-dead person be kept on a respirator to either maintain organs for transplantation, or his body for experimentation?

It depends. Every state has laws[22] that permit the patient, while alive, or the next of kin when he is dead, to make anatomical gifts. If the consent provisions of these laws are met, doctors may maintain the body on a respirator for hours or days or even weeks, for purposes of research or transplantation. It is possible that the next of kin or the deceased's estate would be obligated to pay the cost of maintaining the body while waiting for the anatomical gift to be delivered. Families or patients donating organs might specify, as a condition, that the hospital or recipient pay the costs of maintaining the body during the necessary waiting period.

If the patient or family have not consented to an anatomical gift, the doctor or hospital cannot continue to artificially maintain the body of a brain-dead person. Although doctors have some leeway in deciding when to pronounce such a person dead, they could not, if there is a reasonable basis for suspecting brain death, refrain from turning off the respirator just by delaying the tests that show brain death. Mechanical maintenance of the brain-dead body in such a circumstance, could violate the next of kin's right to have the body turned over for burial, and lead to suits for mutilation of the deceased and emotional distress to the family.[23] In addition, the doctors, rather than the deceased's estate, would be liable for hospital costs incurred after the time that death should have been pronounced and treatment stopped.

Must a doctor maintain a brain-dead person on a respirator if the family insists?

It depends. If the patient or family has made a valid anatomical gift, the doctors and hospital could be found liable if they prevented an organ from being used because they prematurely turned off the respirator.

On the other hand, if maintenance were not essential to effectuate a valid anatomical gift, the doctors and hospital would have no obligation to go on artificially maintaining a brain-dead patient just because the family insisted. If the doctor or hospital were the recipient of the gift and refused it, or if the patient, while alive, had objected to any postmortem organ donation, they would have a right to terminate maintenance over the wishes of the family. Unless there were a specific agreement to do so, the doctor has no duty to promote the survivors' interests, though he could not unreasonably harm their interests. In addition, it is unlikely that courts would hold that the next of kin have a protected interest in having brain-dead bodies kept alive because they think the patient might recover, or because they reject brain-related criteria of death.

NOTES

1. Green and Wikler, *Brain Death and Personal Identity*, 9 Phil. Pub. Aff. 105 (Winter 1980).
2. Black, *Brain Death*, 299 N. Eng. J. Med., 338–44, 397–401 (1978).
3. *A Definition of Irreversible Coma*, 205 J. Amer. Med. Assn. 337–40 (1968).
4. *Black's Law Dictionary* (3d ed.); Thomas v. Anderson, 96 Cal. App. 2d 371, 215 P.2d 478 (1950).
5. For a list of state brain death statutes, see Appendix C.
6. Cal. Health & Safety Code § 7180 (West 1980); Ga. Code Ann. § 88–1715.1 (1979); Ida. Code § 54–1819 (1979).
7. Kan. Stat. Ann. § 77–202, Supp. 1974.
8. *Id.* at 1747.
9. *Id.*
10. *Id.* at 1747–48.
11. President's Commission for the Study of Ethical Problems in Medicine and Biomedical and Behavioral Research, Defining Death, p.2 (July, 1981).
12. New York City Health and Hospital Corporation v. Sulsona, 81 Misc. 2d 1002 (1975).

13. Commonwealth v. Golston, 373 Mass. 249, 366 N.E. 2d 744 (1977). Similar conclusions were reached in Arizona in State v. Fierro, 603 P.2d 74 (Ariz. Banc 1979) and Ohio in State v. Johnson, 381 N.E. 2d 637 (Ohio 1978) aff'g 395 N.E. 2d 368 (Ohio App. 1977).

14. Veith et al, *Brain Death: A Status Report of Legal Considerations*, 238 J. Amer. Med. Assn. 1744, 1746 (1977).

15. *In re* Petition of the Children's Hospital, Inc. No. 49143 (Minn. Dist. Ct., July 11, 1978).

16. Lovato v. District Court, 601 P.2d 1072 (Colo. 1979).

17. *In re* Bowman, 617. P.2d 731 (Wash. Sup. Ct. 1980).

18. See chapter V p 49.

19. See chapter V p 49.

20. Matter of Quinlan, 70 N.J. 10, 355 A.2d 647.

21. Eichner v. Dillon, 426 N.Y.S. 2d 517 (1980).

22. See chapter X, "Organ Transplants and Autopsies"; Waltz and Inbau, *Medical Jurisprudence* 216 (1971).

23. *Id*. at 209–14.

X

Organ Transplants and Autopsies

Patients who a few years ago would die slow and painful deaths from major organ failures, now receive blood, bone marrow, kidney, and heart transplants, which enable them to survive for long periods and lead normal lives. Adoption of brain-related criteria of death has helped the process by making cadaver organs available in a functioning state.

Successful transplants, however, require a supply of transplantable organs. While blood and skin may be available for everyone who needs them, people are less willing to donate other body parts, such as kidneys, hearts, and bone marrow. As a result, many patients who could benefit from organ transplants do not receive them, for the law protects a person's right while alive, and the right of the next of kin when he is dead, to decide whether or not to make an anatomical gift. In the United States, organ donation is not compulsory, and there is no routine salvaging of organs from dead persons.

In addition to the questions of brain death discussed in chapter IX, organ donation and transplants raise two issues for critically ill patients, their doctors, and families— whether the patient has a right to have an organ transplant, and who can determine whether a patient will be used as organ sources for others. Since that issue concerns the control of the body and its parts after death, the question of autopsy is also discussed in this chapter.

Does a critically ill patient have a right to have an organ transplant?

It depends. If an organ is available and the transplant will clearly benefit the patient, he does. This is true whether the patient is a minor, or a competent or incompetent person. For example, a patient who has lost blood would have a right to a blood transfusion, and a burn victim to a skin graft, because these tissues are readily available, and the benefit of receiving them, far outweighs the cost. Doctors who did not use skin grafts and blood transfusions would be regarded as falling below professional standards of care.

Where the risk-benefit ratio is less clear, as with heart, kidney, and marrow transplants, a right to a transplant would exist only if the benefits so clearly outweighed the risks, that customary medical treatment would counsel it. This may be true about kidney, and even heart transplants, in certain circumstances, but often the chances of success and risks are such that doctors will not recommend a transplant. A patient in those circumstances would not have a right to a transplant though he might have a right to be told whether other doctors would recommend this procedure, so that he might consult them. For example, doctors treating end-stage renal disease often differ in their views about the success rate of organ transplants from cadavers and nonrelated donors. Although suits on this issue will be rare, doctors who do not favor transplants probably have a legal obligation to tell their patients that other doctors view the matter differently, so that patients might decide whether to consult them.

Even if a transplant is clearly in the patient's interests, however, she has no right to receive organs, such as a heart or kidneys, that are in short supply. The patient would have to wait his turn in the existing organ allocation system. Legal standards for allocating scarce organs have not yet been established. No cases have yet arisen, and the persons responsible for the system may have no preexisting relation with potential recipients that imposes a legal duty to treat them all equally. Still, it is possible that courts, if ever faced with the issue, would require that minimum standards of fairness be followed in allocating the available supply of organs.

Criteria currently used—length of wait, medical fitness, difficulty with dialysis, and closeness of tissue match—are valid. But criteria related to race, sex, ethnic origin, occupation, or other artibrary factors, would probably not be valid. However, many people would think it fair and nonarbitrary to give a kidney to the parent of six young children, rather than to an institutionalized person with an IQ of 40. Some would also think that it is justifiable to prefer stable, productive members of the community over drug addicts, deviants, or those who contribute less, and whose transplant care is more difficult. However, a community board that selected people for dialysis on the basis of community standing and social worth in Seattle in the late 1960s, when kidney machines were scarce, has been severely criticized.[1]

Lawyers, ethicists, and others writing on the subject, now seem to agree that organs should not be allocated on the basis of a person's social utility.[2] In their view, fairness requires that one's status as a person be respected, aside from the utility that one produces. While exceptions can be made for a narrow class that directly contributes to the health or safety of others, these commentators argue that all persons in need must be treated equally, once criteria of medical fitness have been met. Whether the courts will adopt such standards for organ allocation, is unclear. However, a person who did not receive an organ because of ethnic prejudice, bribery, or some other arbitrary factor, would probably have a good legal claim for damages. Whatever the possible legal repercussions, persons running organ allocation systems should try to make them as fair as possible.

May a critically ill patient decide whether to donate his organs?

Yes. A competent adult, as part of the right of bodily autonomy, has the right to make organ donations to another while he is alive as long as it would not seriously risk his health. Since critically ill patients are unlikely to be sources of organs while they are alive, a more important question is whether they may control use of their body parts after death.

Under the Uniform Anatomical Gift Act in effect in all states, a person eighteen years or older, and of sound mind, has the right to decide whether or not to donate her organs.[3] Under the act, gifts of all, or any part of, the body may be made to: (1) any hospital, surgeon, or physician, for research, or the advancement of medical or dental science, therapy, or transplantation; or (2) any accredited medical or dental school, college, or university, for education, research, or the advancement of medical or dental science or therapy; or (3) any bank or storage facility, for medical or dental education, research, advancement of medical or dental science, therapy, or transplantation.[4]

The donee may accept or reject the gift—a donor has no

legal right to have the donee accept the gift. If accepted, it must be used as specified.[5] (A kidney given to doctors to use in the donor's brother, cannot legally be given to another patient.) If the gift of an organ is accepted, it must be removed without unnecessary mutilation, and the remainder of the body turned over to the surviving spouse or other person responsible for burial. Doctors who act in good faith in giving effect to these gifts after the time of death, are granted immunity from civil or criminal liability (however, immunity does not extend to acts up to, and including, the determination of death).[6]

A person may donate her organs under the act by a provision in her will (the donation provisions take effect immediately upon death), or by signing a card in the presence of two witnesses.[7] As the following form indicates, she can specify which organs are to be donated, and the person or institution to whom they are to be donated. She may also specify how the body is to be buried following its medical use.

UNIFORM DONOR CARD

OF _____
Print or type name of donor

In the hope that I may help others, I hereby make this anatomical gift, if medically acceptable, to take effect upon my death. The words and marks below indicate my desires. I give:

(a) _____ any needed organs or parts

(b) _____ only the following organs or parts

_____
Specify the organ(s) or part(s)

for the purposes of transplantation, therapy, medical research or education;

(c) _____ my body for anatomical study if needed.

Limitations or special wishes, if any: _____

May the family decide about the donation of a critically ill person's body or organs after a person dies?

It depends. If the critically ill person, while alive and competent, had followed the provisions of the Uniform Anatomical Gift Act and made a donation, or has told the family that he objects to such gifts, his wishes control. Under the act, a person's donation of body parts takes effect immediately upon death and is binding on the family.[8] His objection to donation is also binding.[9]

If the deceased has not made a gift or objected to the donation of body parts, then the next of kin has the power to decide whether to make an organ donation. In order of priority among family members for making donation decisions, is the spouse, adult son or daughter, parent, adult brother or sister, guardian at time of death, or any other person authorized or under obligation to dispose of the body.[10] No donation can be made without either the consent of the patient, or the next of kin.

The family of critically ill persons who are close to death (particularly if the person is young, otherwise healthy, and has suffered head or neck injuries in an accident) may be asked by doctors to consent to an organ transplant. If they consent, they will be asked to sign a form stating their consent. This is to protect the hospital and doctors against suits, and serves to remind the family of the choice they are making. The current medical custom is to refrain from telling the family the name of the recipient. The fear is of the social and psychological complications that may arise in the emotionally fraught situation of using the deceased's body to make a possible "gift of life" to another person. While such complications could occur, families often will want to know who will receive the part. The family could refuse to make the donation unless they are told who the recipient will be, though doctors may then seek other donors.

What is the relationship of brain death to organ transplants from critically ill patients?

Brain-related criteria of death, discussed in chapter IX, play a very important role in organ transplantation from cadaveric sources. Brain-related criteria of death enhance the possibility of a successful transplant, because they allow the organs to be artificially maintained in a healthy state until there is a recipient.

Patients and families who consent to organ donations, should remember that the organs will be removed some time after the person has been pronounced dead on brain-related criteria of death. The body's functions will continue to be artificially maintained even after death has been pronounced up until the time that the donated organs are removed. States have adopted brain-related criteria of death in part precisely for this purpose. Death and the time of death in the Anatomical Gift Act would most likely be interpreted to include brain death.[11]

The artificial maintenance of the body while waiting for an appropriate recipient could last several hours or days, and, if a long wait were involved, interfere with funeral arrangements. In one case, a husband who had been told that his wife who was being supported on a respirator after suffering a cerebral hemorrhage was dead, consented to a transplant of her kidneys. When he later learned that her body was kept on the respirator for two more days, he became extremely upset and sued the doctors involved.[12] His suit failed because the doctors had acted in good faith. He had not understood the precise meaning of brain death and that her body might be maintained for some time while waiting for a recipient. A related problem concerns the cost of hospital care during this period. Who pays the cost of such maintenance is unclear, and should be specified in advance so that the family does not incur additional expense.

The close connection between brain death and transplantation has led some people to fear that the need to harvest organs for transplant will influence how and when death is determined, and even deprive patients of medical care that is in their interests to have. The danger is a real one and needs attention. Most states protect against this possibility by legally separating the care of the patient and determination of death, from the transplant procedures.[13] The doctor who pronounces death cannot be involved in the operation. However, an error in the determination of death can occur, even when the decisions are separated. In a Wisconsin case,[14] a potential donor who had been pronounced brain dead, was found to have eye movement on the operating table just before the operation to remove his organs started. The doctors stopped the operation and he eventually recovered. It is thus important that adequate tests of brain death be done to eliminate any error in the diagnosis of death.

May the family prevent a person from donating an organ while he is alive?

No. Conflicts sometimes arise in a family over whether one member should donate an organ. It is not uncommon for a spouse to object to a kidney donation by the other spouse to the donor's brother or sister. However, a person's right of bodily autonomy is controlling here. The family has no legal right to prevent an organ donation. Unless the donation had a high risk of seriously incapacitating or interfering with the donor's ability to carry out other responsibilities, it is unlikely that the courts would permit the family to stop an organ donation by a competent adult, and possibly even a donation by a mature minor.

Can an incompetent patient donate, or be a source of, organs for transplantation while alive?

Yes. If the patient will benefit from the donation, his organs may be transplanted to another. If there is insufficient benefit to the donor, the donation cannot be made, even if necessary to save the life of another person.

This result follows from the basic legal principle that incompetent persons must be protected and cannot be harmed to benefit others. Physical intrusions can occur only if they ultimately benefit the patient. This is an application of the substituted judgment test discussed in chapter V. It recognizes the incompetent person's right of bodily integrity by assuming that the person, if competent and able to express his preferences, would consent only to donations from which he would derive a net benefit, that is, where the benefits outweigh the risks.

Under this test, the consent of incompetent persons to organ transplantations may sometimes be inferred, where a clear benefit to the donor can be shown. This commonly occurs with kidney and bone marrow donations to siblings. In *Strunk* v. *Strunk*,[15] a kidney transplant was made from a mentally retarded twenty-eight-year-old, to his brother, because he would have to be institutionalized if his brother died. The court decided that the benefit to the retarded donor of continued care and contact from his brother, outweighed the low risk of death and temporary discomfort of a kidney donation. Applying the substituted judgment test, it concluded that he would, if able to express his preferences, consent to the donation. Several other courts have reached similar conclusions,[16] and one state, Texas,[17] has legislation authorizing such transplants. However, the contrary result was reached in *Lausier* v. *Pescinski*,[18] where the retarded donor had long been institutionalized, and would not appear to benefit from a donation to a sister and mother of several children, who had not been directly involved with him for many years. As a result, his sister was unable to receive a kidney and eventually died.

Each case involving incompetent donors must, of course, be decided on its own facts. In general, courts have not set impossible standards of determining how the donor would benefit. It is essential, however, that doctors and families receive advance judicial approval before taking an incompetent's organ. An objective determination by an impartial body, with the interests of the incompetent separately represented, is essential, and only a court is well equipped for that function. Taking organs from incompetents without judicial approval runs a great risk of civil and criminal liability and should never occur.

May a minor donate blood, bone marrow, or kidneys, to a critically ill family member?

Yes. The courts have allowed minors to donate organs and tissue to critically ill family members such as brothers and sisters and even parents, when there is no alternative source for the ill member, the benefits to the donor outweigh the risks of donation, and the minor agrees. Thus, a seven-year-old girl donated a kidney to her twin sister who suffered from end-stage renal disease.[19] There was no realistic alternative organ source for the sick sister. Applying substituted judgment, the court found that the donor would suffer grief and possibly feel responsible if her sister died.

Donations of bone marrow and blood have been upheld on the same rationale.[20] In these cases, the child has been able to demonstrate an understanding of the nature of the donation, and the consequences if the donation is not allowed. If the child is too young to understand the procedure, courts may still permit the transplant if a clear benefit that outweighs the risk to the donor, is established. In these cases, however, advance judicial approval is required to protect minors who are unable to protect themselves from exploitation or manipulation. A guardian *ad litem* will be appointed for the minor, and the need for the child's organ and possibility of benefit will be closely scrutinized.

Can a person be compelled to donate tissue or organs to a close family member?

No. Parents, spouses, and siblings, as well as other less closely related family members, have no legal obligation to donate tissue or organs. A person's right of bodily integrity includes the right not to have body parts taken without consent, even if the intrusion is relatively minor, and a substantial benefit, such as saving life, will be conferred on a close member of the family.

The strongest case for a compelled donation would be from parent to child. There is a precedent for imposing surgery on a woman to preserve the life of a full-term fetus (see the discussion of forced Caesarean sections in chapter IV, p. 32), and the interests of minors may outweigh a parent's right to refuse necessary medical treatments. However, with the exception of a compelled blood donation, or some other similar minimal intrusion, it is highly unlikely that a parent's duty to provide a child with medical care would include a duty to offer one's own body parts where a significant risk is involved. In the absence of legislation, a court probably would not order a parent to donate a kidney to save his child's life, though it might compel the parent to donate blood or bone marrow, or receive a transfusion to protect the child. A law authorizing courts to order body donations from parents to children in very restricted circumstances—where the compelled donation involved low risk, and would confer a great benefit on the recipient unavailable through other means—could possibly be found to be constitutional. However, no such law currently exists, and in the current climate of opinion, is unlikely to be passed.

A case that firmly upheld the principles of individual autonomy and bodily integrity occurred when a man suffering from immune system deficiency asked the court to order his brother to donate bone marrow that would help regenerate his immune system and enable him to live.[21] The brother seemed to be the only available source of bone marrow that matched his tissue type. The court denied the suit, holding that if the donor objected, there was no duty to provide body organs or tissue, even when the risk to the donor was small, and it was necessary to save the life of the recipient.

Who decides whether an autopsy will occur?

An autopsy is an examination of the deceased's body to determine the cause of death. For medical, scientific, and educational reasons, doctors and hospitals try to do as many autopsies on deceased patients as possible, and will often ask the next of kin for permission soon after death is pronounced. Unless murder or suicide is suspected, and laws requiring autopsies apply, the next of kin ordinarily has the sole right to decide whether this will occur.[22] The family confronted with such a request should remember that autopsies do not leave the body mutilated or unfit for viewing in a funeral service. They serve valid scientific and medical purposes, and often can determine the precise cause of death. But the wishes of survivors are important here, and are protected by the law. Many suits have been won for the emotional suffering inflicted on survivors who did not consent to an autopsy.

An important exception to the family's right to decide on an autopsy is the patient's right to donate his body for research purposes under the Uniform Anatomical Gift Act. In addition, a few states provide for advance consent to an autopsy while alive.[23] If the patient has executed a document permitting an autopsy under these laws, it is binding on relatives. (His objection to an autopsy would probably not be binding on them, because their authority to consent exists independently of the Uniform Anatomical Gift Act.) However, few patients consent to an autopsy in advance, perhaps because few doctors are willing to broach the subject with critically ill patients.

NOTES

1. Dukeminier and Sanders, *Medical Advances and Legal L: Hemodialysis and Kidney Transplantation*, 15 U.C.L.A. L. Rev. 537 (1968).
2. Katz, *Process Design for Selection of Hemodialysis and Organ Transplant Recipients*, 22 Buff. L. Rev. 373 (1973). A. Winslow, *Triangle and Justice* (1982).
3. Section 2, in Waltz and Inbau, *Medical Jurisprudence* 220 (1971).
4. *Id.*
5. *Id.*
6. *Id.*
7. *Id.*
8. *Id.*
9. *Id.*

10. *Id.*
11. New York City Health and Hospital Corporation v. Solsona, 81 Misc. 2d 1002 (1975).
12. Williams v. Hofmann, 66 Wis. 2d 145, 223 N.W. 2d 844 (1974).
13. Section 7(b) of the Uniform Anatomical Gift Act. See Waltz and Inbau, *Medical Jurisprudence* 220 (1971).
14. Dead UW Official Blinks As Doctors Start To Operate, *Capitol Times*, Madison, Wis., Feb. 13, 1975, p.1.
15. Strunk v. Strunk, 445 S.W. 2d 145 (Ky. 1969).
16. See, e.g., Little v. Little, 576 S.W. 2d 49 (Tex. Ct. Civil Appeals, 1979).
17. TEX. REV. CIV. STAT. ANN. art. 4590–2a (Vernon Supp. 1980).
18. Lausier v. Pescinski, 67 Wis. 2d 4, 226 N.W. 2d 180 (1975). See also *In re* Richardson, 284 So. 2d 185 (La. Ct. App.), *cert. denied*, 284 So. 2d 338 (La. 1973).
19. Hart v. Brown, 29 Conn. Super. 368, 289 A.2d 386 (Super. Ct. 1972). See also cases summarized in Curran, *A Problem of Consent: Kidney Transplants in Minors*, 34 N.Y.U. L. Rev. 891 (1959).
20. Baron, Botsford, and Cole, *Live Organ and Tissue Transplants from Minor Donors in Massachusetts*, 55 B.U. L. Rev. 159 (1975).
21. McFall v. Shrimp, No. 78–17711 In Equity (C.P. Allegheny County, Pa., July 26, 1978); Meisel, *Must a Man Be His Cousin's Keeper?* 8 Hastings Center Report 5 (1978).
22. Waltz and Inbau, *Medical Jurisprudence*, 204–14 (1971).
23. Annas, *The Rights of Hospital Patients*, 175 (1975).

XI

Experimentation and the Critically Ill

Critically ill patients and their families may often be faced with questions of medical experimentation. These are most likely to arise if the patient is treated in a hospital affiliated with a medical school (a "teaching hospital"). Doctors on the staff, including those directly caring for patients, may conduct research to improve treatment and gain new knowledge. Doctors may approach critically ill patients or their families, if they are incompetent, and invite them to be research subjects. Questions of experimentation are also likely to arise when a patient seeks a therapy or treatment not in general use.

Participation in research may often be in a patient's interest—it might prolong life, reduce pain, or give the patient the satisfaction of knowing he's helping others. In many instances, however, experimental therapies may have no therapeutic benefit and may involve serious side effects. Also, the patient's well-being may conflict with the needs of the study. The potential for this conflict is greatest when a doctor conducts research on patients he's also treating.

In the last fifteen years, an elaborate system for protecting research subjects, including strict rules of informed consent and approval by an institutional review board (IRB) has developed.[1] The rights of research subjects are now legally recognized. Patients are protected from unwanted research, and have a greater chance of participating in a satisfying research venture with the doctor.

Does a critically ill patient have a right not to be a research subject?

Yes. Researchers are required by state law, federal regulations, and codes of professional ethics, to have the free, informed consent of competent subjects or their guardians, if incompetent, before conducting research on them.[2] They cannot penalize patients who refuse, by denying them the care that they would otherwise receive. This requirement applies to all forms of research, including interviewing or photographing such patients, as well as testing drugs or other medical procedures. A Maine court, for example, has allowed damages to be imposed on a surgeon who took photographs over the objections of a patient dying from neck cancer, even though the photographs were to benefit science and future patients.[2A] However, a doctor could refuse to treat a patient who refuses to participate in research, as long as the patient could arrange adequate care elsewhere. Where certain drugs or treatments are available only as part of an experiment, a person may have to consent to be a research subject in order to get the treatment.

What if the patient is incompetent and cannot consent?

Although state courts have not yet dealt directly with this question, they are likely to accept the principles for research with incompetents developing on the federal level. These principles allow research to be done on incompetent subjects if an IRB approves the research, the patient's guardian gives informed consent, and the research will benefit the incompetent patient, by possibly prolonging his life.[3] The guardian may also consent to nonbeneficial research that has minimal risk or is not greatly intrusive.[4] Nonbeneficial research of more than minimal risk cannot be done, even with the consent of the guardian, due to the harm it would inflict on the incompetent patient.

Guardians are not always appointed for incompetent patients due to the reluctance of many doctors to go to the courts to appoint a guardian, instead they will ask the permission of the family. If the family acts solely in the interests of the incompetent, and the research is beneficial or offers only minimal risk, the consent of the next of kin may be legally sufficient. Where the research is highly risky, a more desirable course of action would be to have a guardian appointed to give consent. This will protect the interests of the incompetent patient, and protect the doctors against later legal challenges.

May critically ill children participate in research?

Yes. Again the principles and rules developing for federally funded research are likely to be legally recognized by state courts faced with questions about the legality of research with children. Generally, the federal rules that apply to incompetent adults apply to children, unless the child is mature enough to consent for himself.[5] In addition to institutional requirements for all research, such as IRB approval, the consent of parents and guardians would be required, and the research would have to be beneficial for the child. If nonbeneficial, only minimal risk, and not greatly invasive, research could be done. Federal regulations for research with children leave the question of the child's assent or consent to the IRB.[6]

If the child is mature enough to understand the risks and benefits of the proposed research, he may be competent to decide on his own. In that case, he could not be used without his informed consent. Depending on the extent to which the minor has a right to determine his medical care without parental consent, he may have a right to participate, even if his parents object.[7] In research involving more than minimal risk, researchers should still try to get the consent of parents of mature minors until the law is clarified, even though it might not turn out to be legally required. If the parents object, researchers should not proceed without judicial clarification of the minor's right to participate in research.

If a person consents to be a subject, may she change her mind?

Yes. The federal rules for experimentation permit a subject not to enter the research at all, or once having entered, to withdraw at any time, for any reason without penalty.[8] A guardian who consents for an incompetent patient may also withdraw consent after the research has started. Consent forms for research usually state this right, though it exists whether or not stated in the form. In cases where the subject is paid, however, withdrawal after beginning the research, may affect the payment.

Does a person have a right to be paid for being a research subject?

No, unless the researcher has specifically promised to pay for participation. Critically ill patients are usually asked to volunteer without pay—to contribute their time and bodies for the sake of medical science or for a possible therapeutic benefit. In many cases, there may be no benefit to the subject, other than the satisfaction of contributing to research. In other cases, there may be some therapeutic benefit that would not be available otherwise, as is the case if a new cancer drug was legally available only in research.

What must a person be told in order to give informed consent to research?

Federal research regulations for informed consent require that the subject must be told the nature and purpose of the research, the right not to participate without penalty, the right to withdraw at any time, the right to ask questions, and the extent of compensation if injured. In addition, she must be told the risks and benefits of the proposed experiment, and alternatives.[9] Unless the research involves a very small risk, this information must be written in a consent form. The patient has a right to keep a copy of this form. State law is likely to follow the federal requirements for informed consent. In some cases, however, state law may even be stricter, requiring that any information relating to the decision of a person in the subject's circumstances, be disclosed.[10]

Patients asked to take part in research should remember that they have a right to receive detailed information about the risks, danger, or inconveniences (if any) as well as the benefits of participation. If they are unclear, or if they do not understand, they should ask the researcher for more information before consenting. If the patient does not believe that the research is in her interest, or has doubts concerning its benefits, she is free to decide without penalty, not to take part.

Will a person injured in research have his medical expenses and other losses paid?

Contrary to the belief of many subjects, no.

If injuries occur without negligence, there is no legal right to compensation, even if the injury leads to substantial medical expenses and lost earnings. While many people argue that the researcher or research institution should pay for these losses, few do. In fact, the general practice has been not to inform subjects that they will bear these costs when they occur. Federal regulations now require that subjects be told in advance whether they will be compensated for injuries or not.[11] A presidential commission studying the problem, has recommended a pilot study of compensation for nonnegligent research-related injuries. However, not all research injuries may be covered by such a scheme, particularly those suffered by critically ill patients whose illness could produce injuries similar to those caused by the research.[12]

Even if injury does not occur, the research could increase the patient's hospital bill, because research often involves extra medical expenses.[13] Patients should be told in advance if the research will increase their bill so they can take it into account in deciding whether to participate. If nothing is said, they should ask the doctor. They may refuse to participate if such costs exist and they do not wish to pay for them.

Does a critically ill patient have a right to participate in research?

No. Doctors are free to select as subjects the persons whom they think are most useful to the research. They are not obligated to offer an experimental therapy to all patients, or to honor the wishes of all persons who want to be subjects.

In some cases, however, a doctor may be obligated to inform a patient that a new or experimental therapy is being used by some doctors, or preferred by some patients. For example, doctors who think that radical mastectomy is the best treatment for breast cancer, would have to tell their patients that other doctors think that simple mastectomy, a less expensive operation, is just as effective even if still being used experimentally, so that patients might have the chance to decide for themselves whether they would prefer to seek out the experimental therapy.

A patient would have a right to participate in research if the doctor is willing, and the research is otherwise lawful. Even then, however, the hospital may require that an experimentation review committee or IRB review and approve the research before it is done.

Must the patient's family consent to her participation in research?

It depends. If the patient is competent she is free to decide to participate in research and her spouse or family cannot stop her. (An institutional review board, however, could disapprove the research on other grounds.)

If the patient is incompetent, research generally cannot be

done without the consent of the patient's guardian. If there is no guardian, the next of kin will usually be asked to consent for the patient. The guardian or next of kin may only consent if the research is likely to benefit the incompetent patient, or which, if nonbeneficial, offers only minimal risk. They have no legal authority to permit research that poses more than minimal risk to an incompetent subject.[14]

What is a randomized clinical trial?

A randomized clinical trial is a method of testing a new treatment by randomly assigning patients to the new treatment or to a control group. In order to get scientifically valid results, the control group might receive the standard, conventional therapy which doctors are trying to improve, or no therapy, usually in the form of a pill called a placebo. The patients will not know in advance whether they will be assigned to the new treatment, or to the control group, since the random assignment occurs only after they have consented to participate.

In some cases it will also be "double-blind." This means that neither the researcher nor the subject will know who has received the new treatment until the experiment is over. This method is used to prevent bias in interpreting the results.

Does a patient have a right to know whether he is part of a randomized clinical trial?

Yes. The patient or guardian must give their consent. If they were not part of the study, the patient would have a right to have the standard therapy and be told of alternative or new therapies. By participating in a random clinical trial, however, a subject loses this choice. Instead, he has a fifty-percent chance of getting an untested, possibly harmful, or possibly beneficial treatment, rather than the best available standard treatment. Patients must be told of this possibility, so that they might make an informed choice.

Patients should also remember that by consenting to be a research subject in a randomized clinical trial, there's no guarantee that they will get the new treatment. Those subjects in the control group who receive the standard therapy, or placebo, are still part of the research, even though they do not receive the new treatment.

Is it in a patient's interest to be in a randomized clinical trial?

It depends. Often it will be in the patient's interest because there will not be enough scientific evidence to know whether the experimental or standard therapy is better. If all other things are equal, choosing randomly is a rational way to decide on treatment. It is also essential to obtain scientifically valid information about the treatment, so that other patients may benefit in the future.

However, in some instances, the treatment may not be exactly equal. Data that suggests that one treatment is better than another may lead some doctors and patients, in situations of uncertainty and great risk, to choose it over the other, even though their judgment is not scientifically based, and more research is needed. Such persons would not find randomization in their interest, for it presents a fifty-percent chance that they will not receive the treatment that they prefer. One of the two treatments may also have less tolerable side effects than the other.

Because a patient might prefer to get a treatment directly, and not take a fifty-percent risk of getting the less desirable one, patients should ask their doctor or researcher about the relative desirability of the treatment being offered in the experiment. If one seems more desirable, because it seems more likely to be efficacious, or has fewer side effects, they should then ask whether they may get it directly from their doctor or from another doctor, without being in the research.

Can a patient get an experimental drug or treatment without becoming a research subject?

In many cases, yes. Often research will be done to test drugs and treatments that are already being used by some doctors to treat patients, even though not yet accepted universally because their efficacy has not been established scientifically. A patient could get the new treatment without being part of a study by going directly to those doctors who are already using it. Some patients might prefer to rely on the new, untested treatment and get it directly, for a patient offered the treatment in a random clinical trial has only a 50-50 chance of getting the new treatment. In other circumstances, however, the new treatment may be legally available only in a research setting.

Can experimentation be carried out on a brain-dead person?

Yes. If the deceased has specifically agreed to such research while alive, or the next of kin consents, such research would appear to be lawful.

Doctors may be interested in studying physical functions or procedures in critically ill patients which cannot ethically or legally be done while the person is alive because they are incompetent and the research has more than minimal risk, or because it is difficult to recruit subjects while alive. When the person is legally dead, the legal and ethical obstacles to experimenting on a live person no longer exist and the body may be physically maintained in a way that allows the research to occur.

Under the Uniform Anatomical Gift Act, such research would be lawful if proper consent has been obtained. The act authorizes gifts of "all or any part of (the) body . . . for medical or dental education, research, or advancement of medical or dental science."[15] This language would encompass research on brain-dead persons, as long as the provisions of the act for making such gifts, is followed. These provisions are the same for making organ donations (see chapter X). If the deceased had not consented while alive, the appropriate next of kin would have to give consent. Unless such research were found to be so offensive that the present law would have to to be changed, research on the brain dead is clearly legal as long as the proper consent has been obtained.

It is not clear whether such research would have to be approved by the hospital research review committee or IRB. The federal research regulations, which apply only to human subjects, do not apply to research on the dead,[16] and thus would not require such review. However, the institution's own policies might require prior review by an IRB. Researchers considering using brain-dead subjects, should check with their IRB before proceeding.

NOTES

1. Katz, *Experimentation with Human Beings* (1972). 45 Code of Federal Regulations, §§ 46.101–.301 (1977).

2. Annas, Glantz, and Katz, *Informed Consent to Human Experimentation*, 27–55 (1977).

2A. Berthiaume's Estate v. Pratt, 365 A.2d 792 (Me. 1976).

3. *Id.* at 63–76. National Commission for Protection of Human Subjects of Biomedical and Behavioral Research, Research Involving those Institutionalized as Mentally Infirm, DHEW Publication No. (05) 78–0006 (1978).
4. *Id.* at 7–28.
5. National Commission for Protection of Human Subjects of Biomedical and Behavioral Research, Research Involving Children, DHEW Publication No. (05)77–0004 (1977). See also Annas, Glantz, and Katz, *Informed Consent to Human Experimentation*, 63–94 (1977).
6. 45 CFR 46.409(a).
7. Bellotti v. Baird, 443 U.S. 622 (1979).
8. 45 CFR § 46.103(c).
9. *Id.;* see also Annas, Glantz and Katz, *Informed Consent to Human Experimentation*, 27–38.
10. Canterbury v. Spence, 464 F.2d 772 (D.C. Cir. 1972).
11. 45 CFR 46.116(a)(b).
12. See President's Commission for the Study of Ethical Problems in Medicine and Biomedical and Behavioral Research, *Compensating For Research Injuries*, 106–110 (June, 1982).
13. Robertson, Ten Ways to Improve IRBs, The Hastings Center, Report, 29, 31, Fed. 1979.
14. See notes 3 and 5.
15. Waltz and Inbau, *Medical Jurisprudence*, 220–24 (1971).
16. Robertson, "Case Study: Research with the Brain Dead," 2 *IRB: A Journal of Human Subject Research*, 4–6 (Apr. 1980).

XII

Costs and Allocation of Scarce Resources

Critical illness is very expensive in the United States. Of the nine percent of the GNP that goes to health care annually, a large portion goes to critical illness—to intensive care units, trauma centers, doctors' fees, dialysis, and the ever-mounting costs of long, intensive, chronic care.

These enormous costs have important implications for the treatment and medical care given to critically ill patients, and for the families, physicians, hospitals, and welfare agencies involved in their care. The financial effect of critical illness can devastate a patient and his family—it can deplete all of one's resources and even cause bankruptcy. The costs may be so great that some persons may not be able to get doctors or hospitals to treat them. It thus raises the question of whether the government has a duty to, or at least should, help pay the costs of catastrophic illness.

In the final analysis, the question of costs involves difficult moral, social, and political choices about how to allocate scarce medical resources. Tragic choices must be faced concerning the grounds for denying treatment to some patients, in order to conserve resources for others. This chapter discusses some of the legal issues that arise from the high costs of critical illness, and their implication for treatment decisions by patients, families, doctors, hospitals, and government.

Who pays the costs of critical illness?

The patient is legally obligated to pay the costs of medical treatment during his critical illness. About seventy percent of Americans have some form of health insurance which will cover some or all of these costs. If the patient does not have

146

health insurance or it runs out, he is personally liable to pay the rest. If he dies, his estate is liable for unpaid medical bills. The family is not obligated to pay the patient's bills, unless the patient is a minor, or unless they have independently agreed to do so during the course of the illness.

If the patient is unable to pay (because he is indigent, or has depleted all his funds and insurance), various governmental programs may pay all or some of the costs of his treatment. For patients over sixty-five, for example, Medicare will pay a significant portion. In most states, Medicaid will pay the costs of patients who do not qualify for Medicare, and who are indigent. Persons with end-stage renal disease will have nearly all the costs of kidney transplant or dialysis, paid for under Medicare. (The details of the Medicare and Medicaid coverage are covered in *The Rights of Older Persons*.) State and local governments may provide emergency medical services free of charge, or run municipal or state hospitals that give free care to the critically or chronically ill.

Finally, some private, voluntary hospitals will accept patients who are unable to pay under the Hill-Burton Act.[1] Under this program, hospitals which have received federal funds for hospital construction, are obligated to provide, on an annual basis, up to three percent of their operating costs or ten percent of the federal assistance received in free medical care to indigents. Indigent patients must be informed of this possibility, and should inquire if they think they qualify.

Is the government obligated to provide health-care for critically ill patients?

No. There is no constitutional right to have the government provide health care. The government has, through Medicare, Medicaid, and some other programs, undertaken to do so. As a result, a person who meets the qualifications of those programs, has a right to the funds which they provide.

It should be noted that the government is not obligated to fund all medically necessary procedures in the programs that it does support. It may, for example, not fund abortions, even though it funds other medically necessary procedures.[2] It may fund all the costs of one disease category, such as end-stage renal disease, without also funding the costs of hemophilia. In 1980, for example, the government decided to discontinue payments for heart transplants under Medicare.[3] It based its decision on a combination of factors—the uncertain efficacy of heart transplants, the difficulty in selecting patients fairly, and the enormous cost (about $35,000), which could be spent in ways that would help more patients.[4]

Is a patient's family obligated to pay the costs of his critical illness?

Generally, no. A family member, even a spouse, is not legally obligated to pay a family member's hospital bills. However, these would be considered claims against the estate of a deceased person, and must be paid before any money can be inherited by family members. If the patient recovers, and has not been declared bankrupt, then these would be claims against further earnings or income.

In three situations family members may be liable for the costs of critical illness. Where the patient is a child, parents have a legal obligation, unless they have terminated parental rights, to pay the medical costs of their children. They are obligated to pay the costs, often enormous, that critical illness in children incurs. This obligation continues even if they refuse to consent to the treatment, as sometimes arises with handicapped children.[5] Secondly, in some states, a spouse will be obligated to pay the debts of another spouse.[6] Finally, the family can be liable if they have cosigned or agreed to pay costs as an initial condition of treatment, or entry into the hospital.

Can a patient be refused admission to a hospital if he is unable to pay?

Yes and no. If the indigent patient is brought to the emergency room of a hospital and needs emergency care, then he cannot be refused for inability to pay, since hospitals may not turn people away in such circumstances. However, once the emergency is over, the hospital is not obligated to admit him. Municipal hospitals cannot refuse to treat indigent patients. Voluntary hospitals can, though in some cases, under the provisions of the Hill-Burton Act, they may be obligated to provide free services to indigents. Voluntary hospitals may even refuse to accept patients whose bills will be paid by Medicaid.

Can a patient be discharged from a hospital if she is unable to pay?

Probably not. Although there is no obligation to admit the patient once emergency care is provided, once a patient has been admitted and needs continued hospitalization, the hospital probably cannot discharge her solely because of a predicted inability to pay. Thus, patients cannot simply be discharged if their health insurance or Medicare or Medicaid coverage has run out, if this will injure their health. However, the hospital can have the patient transferred to another facility, if one is available, that will meet the patient's needs.

This situation frequently arises because a hospital is required to periodically review each Medicare patient to determine whether the hospital stay is warranted. If not, Medicare will no longer pay the hospital costs. In such cases, the hospital would prefer to discharge the patient, and will try to have the patient transferred to a nursing home or an intermediate care facility which Medicare will cover. If such a facility is not available, the hospital will have to continue to care for the patient, even if Medicare will not reimburse the costs. If the patient is improperly discharged for inability to pay, and suffers injury as a result, a civil suit for damages for abandonment could probably be successfully brought by patients with the will and resources to assert their rights.

May a doctor refuse to treat a patient who is unable to pay?
Yes. Doctors, unlike hospitals, have no legal obligation to anyone. They may refuse to treat a patient because of inability to pay, or for any other reason, even arbitrary ones. For example, a South Carolina doctor was able legally to refuse to treat welfare patients (whose bills were paid by Medicaid) if they refused to agree to be sterilized after their third child.[7] Similarly, privately run centers that receive federal funds for dialysis, can decide which new patients to accept, thus leaving the sickest and most disruptive patients to be treated by others. One exception to this rule arises when the doctor is on the staff of, or is an employee of, a hospital or facility which undertakes to treat others. By virtue of his employment contract, that physician would be obligated to treat anyone entitled to care in that hospital.

May a doctor stop treating a patient who is unable to pay?
It depends. Although not obligated to begin treatment, once this is undertaken, he is obligated to continue as long as the patient will benefit or the patient withdraws. A refusal to treat is abandonment and can lead to civil damages if the patient is injured as a result of the refusal.

The effect of a patient's failure to pay on the doctor's obligation not to abandon his patient is unclear. If the doctor has made payment a specific condition of further treatment, she may be able to stop treatment on this basis. If the physician has not made ability to pay an explicit condition of continuing treatment, it is less likely that the courts will permit the doctor to defend himself against a charge of abandonment when the patient has been injured by the refusal. However, if the patient has time to obtain other medical services, a doctor probably could refuse the patient further treatment because of inability to pay. The result is that while a doctor cannot abandon a patient in the middle of treatment because of inability to pay, he is not obligated to provide every medical service which the patient needs. If the government or insurers have decided not to pay for those services, the doctor caring for the patient is not obligated to provide them at her own expense.

May the government refuse to fund medical procedures because they are too expensive and might benefit too few people.

Yes. There is no question that the state or private insurers may refuse to fund certain services or patient groups because of the great cost involved. The government has no constitutional obligation to fund health care at all, and may choose to fund some, but not all, services. Medicare and Medicaid, for example, do not fund medically necessary abortions or heart transplants.[8] It could choose to cut back on the coverage of renal dialysis, just as it has eliminated neighborhood health centers for the poor.

In the future, as the costs of health care continue to mount, we may expect to see the government take a much harder look at the cost-benefit ratio of many funded health services. It is likely that the government will refuse to fund procedures from which an individual patient could benefit, but which from a societal perspective, appear to be too costly. Too few patients may benefit, or the procedure may prolong life but not return patients to normal functioning, to justify the cost when the same funds could help more people in other ways. Some patients will die because they are unable to pay, and the state is unwilling to pay, for the very expensive care that they require. While many of these decisions will be cloaked in such terms as not being "medically necessary," or "not medi-

cally indicated," the brute fact, unescapably in a world of
scarce resources, is that funds to prolong a person's life will
not always be available.[9] *why should they be*

May physicians and hospitals refuse to treat patients because they think a procedure is too expensive in light of its benefits?

The answer is unclear, and depends on the extent of the
physician's right to ration medical care according to his view
of the best use of medical resources.

The situation at issue here, arises when the services in
question will be paid (either by the patient, private insurers,
or the government), yet the physician thinks it is wasteful or
unnecessary to provide them. As long as a respectable portion, even a minority of the medical community agrees that
the procedure is "unnecessary," in light of its costs and
benefits, the physician would not be liable for not providing
them. In effect, the law will recognize the doctor's authority
to ration social resources in the guise of judgments of "medical benefit" and "reasonable and necessary services."[10]

However, a doctor who decides not to provide a service on
rationing or resource allocation grounds, should inform a
patient of the grounds of her decision and the possibility that
he may be able to obtain it from another doctor.[11] In those
states (about a quarter) that follow the informed consent rule
that a doctor must disclose all information that the patient
would need to know to make a decision, a doctor could be
liable if he failed to provide this information. In the professional custom states (the other three fourths), the doctor
would not be liable for nondisclosure as long as other doctors
did not also disclose the basis for their decisions.

How must patients be selected for a drug, a procedure, a hospital bed, or other service that is in short supply?

Selection depends on the judgment of the physicians
involved, as long as they are not using a patently arbitrary
standard for their choice.

The problem of selection for treatment when there is scarcity arises in two situations other than funding decisions by
government or private insurers. One such situation arises
when there is a sudden increase in demand for medical
services which available facilities cannot meet—in wartime,
mass disasters, or accidents with multiple victims. In emergency

situations, where not all lives can be saved, doctors are free to practice "triage," and choose according to a standard that reflects generally held community values, such as treating those most likely to survive or those whose treatment will enable the greatest number of persons to be saved.[12] While the ethics of choice in those situations are quite complex,[12] it is unlikely that the courts would hold a physician liable who made a good faith judgment about how best to maximize patient welfare in such circumstances unless corruption or clearly unacceptable standards, such as racist, religious, or sexist bias, were used to make the decision.

The second situation concerns nonemergency situations when a drug, an organ for transplant, or a bed in an intensive care unit, is in short supply. Although the courts have not yet dealt with this issue, it's very probable that the law will allow the physicians involved to make the judgment about how best to use the scarce resource, as long as they are not made on clearly impermissible grounds.

Aside from instances where a patient might have a prior claim to the scarce resource because the physician has been treating him, doctors are free to allocate the resource to those who are likely to survive the longest in the best quality of life, even though others would gain a personal benefit from its use. They could choose to give the kidney or heart or drug to the otherwise healthiest person, rather than to the one who is dying, or who lacks the psychological ability to handle the demands of the treatment. They can also allocate according to a principle wherein many patients would be helped, rather than a very few, or allocate according to the needs of clinical research. Although heart transplants cannot be done on a racially discriminatory basis, they can probably legally be denied to the very sick and the retarded.

Of course, such allocation decisions implicate very basic values, and are ethically debatable. The law, however, is not likely to punish doctors, either civilly or criminally, for their rationing decisions unless blatantly corrupt or arbitrary standards are used. While it is possible that legislation setting standards for these decisions will be passed at some point, the moral dilemmas that they raise are so painful and difficult to resolve openly, that societal reliance on doctors to make them in the guise of clinical judgment, is likely to continue.

To summarize, in situations of scarcity where triage, or the selection of a few for treatment from which many can benefit, must be made, no individual patient has a legal right to be selected over any other patient. A doctor's clinical judgment about how best to use a scarce resource will be legally recognized. A patient only has a right not to be discriminated against on racial, sexual, or other patently arbitrary grounds.

NOTES

1. Hill-Burton Act.
2. Beal v. Doe, 432 U.S. 438; Maher v. Roe, 432 U.S. 464; Poelker v. Doe, 432 U.S. 519; McCrae v. Harris, 448 U.S. 297 (1980).
3. 45 Fed. Reg. 52296–97, Aug. 8, 1980.
4. Knox, *Heart Transplants: To Pay or Not to Pay*, 209 Science 570–74, Aug. 1980.
5. See chapter VI, p. 71.
6. See, e.g., ARIZ. REV. STAT. § 13–3611 (1978).
7. Walker v. Pierce, 560 F.2d 609 (4th Cir. 1977).
8. See notes 3 and 4.
9. For an account of this problem, see Calabrese and Bobbitt, *Tragic Choices* (1978).
10. Blumstein, *constitutional and Legal Constraints on the Rationing of Medical Resources*, 59 Tex. L. Rev. 1345 (1982).
11. *Id.* at 1392–1395.
12. G. Winslow, *Triage and Justice*, 85–86, 105–109 (1982).

XIII

Hospices

Most Americans die in the impersonal atmosphere of hospitals, surrounded by aggressive medical treatment and technology that may prevent them, as well as their families, from dealing adequately with the psychological realities of dying. Dissatisfaction with this situation has fostered a movement to help patients and their families confront death in supportive nonhospital settings, with a minimum of medical care. Central to the movement are hospice programs which provide palliative and supportive care to patients and their families in the dying process, and which try to encourage dying at home.

Although the notion of a hospice for dying patients has deep historical roots, the main inspiration for its development in the United States, has come from St. Christopher's Hospice in London,[1] which, in the last ten years, has become a model for the care of the terminally ill. Hospice programs modeled on St. Christopher's now exist or are being planned in nearly every state.[2] They are attractive to patients and families because of their concern with the psychosocial realities of dying and the rights of patients, and to health-planners, insurers, and policymakers, because they cost less than hospital care. The hospice movement may turn out to be a significant development in the care of the critically ill in America. Although legal disputes over patient rights have seldom arisen, and may never play a large role in the hospice setting, questions of patient rights can become an issue. This chapter discusses legal issues relevant to hospice care.

154

What is a hospice?

A hospice is a program of home and institutional care that provides palliative and supportive care for terminally ill patients and their families. Hospices have grown up in response to the inability of most hospitals and nursing homes to meet the physical, psychological, and social problems of the patient and the next of kin in the dying process. Hospice programs focus on patients dying from incurable, degenerative diseases for whom aggressive, curative treatment has ceased to be beneficial. They openly face the reality of the patient's impending death and, through palliative and supportive care turned to the particular needs of the patient, try to "help the patient 'live' while dying."[3] Pain is aggressively alleviated by prescribing medication on a preventive, rather than an as needed basis, without regard to addictive potential, thus reducing the anxiety patients feel when they fear that their pain cannot be controlled. Emotional, spiritual, psychological, and physical care is provided. The goal is to allow the patient maximum control of the care he receives. Most hospices are sensitive to the loneliness and isolation that many dying patients feel, and make care available twenty-four hours a day, seven days a week.

To enable the patient to live as normal a life as possible, most hospices provide home care. At any given time more hospice patients are living at home, than in the hospice facility.[4] When a facility is used (which could be free standing or a special wing of a hospital), it tries to be as homelike as possible in appearance, access by family and friends, and concern for the needs of patients.

In keeping with the hospice's emphasis on the psychosocial needs of patients and their families, the staff is interdisciplinary and specially trained in the needs of the dying. While physicians often head the hospice team, nonmedical skills are equally important. Clergy, nurses, social workers, and community volunteers, as well as family and friends, provide care to the dying.

Family involvement is a central feature of hospice programs. Most hospices regard the family and close friends of the patient, as well as the patient, as the unit of care. It welcomes family members, including children, in the hospice facility and tries to enlist them in the caring process. The staff helps families understand and cope with their own reactions to a dying relative, thus enabling the family to care for the patient at home without being overburdened.

Do patients go to hospices to die?

Some might, and some might die there. However, the hospice concept is based on the idea that "a dying person should be allowed to finish her life at home, surrounded by a concerned family, amid her own possessions, and in a setting that can maximize physical and psychological comfort."[5] Hospices have fewer beds than patients. Most patients are cared for at home through visits from hospice staff or outpatient care at the hospice facility. However, a patient may enter a hospice facility to supplement home care when his physical needs require closer attention, or when there is no one to assist at home. Such persons might die in the hospice. Or, a dying person may go to a hospice for a short period to give family members temporary relief from the stress of caring for a dying person. During the course of a terminal illness, there may be one or more periods of residency in a hospice facility, but in a successful hospice program most patients will die at home.

Do patients have a right to be admitted to a hospice?

No. Since hospices exist to serve the needs of dying patients, they try to serve the needs of as many people as their program permits. However, they have no legal obligation to accept every patient who applies. A hospice program may, for example, offer to arrange for home care rather than admit a certain patient, or not offer any services at all to certain patient groups. Some hospice programs, for example, deal only with terminal cancer, and not other degenerative diseases. Most deal with adult and elderly problems, and may not be equipped to deal with dying adolescents and children.

It is possible that if a hospice undertook to provide home care services, it would have a legal obligation to admit patients to its facility when care could no longer be provided at home. But no cases have been brought against hospices, and given the philosophy of hospice care, few cases are likely.

Can a doctor be sued for not informing or referring a patient to an available hospice program?

Possibly, though no case has yet arisen. The case for recovery would be strongest if referral to hospice programs became a standard medical practice for dying patients and the attending doctor neglected to do so, causing the patient to receive more medical care, hospitalization, and pain and suffering than he otherwise would. In such a case, the patient or family could argue that their consent to further medical treatment was not based on full disclosure, since information about an available hospice program had been withheld and they would have chosen the hospice program if informed of it. While liability is theoretically possible, damages may be too small to justify the costs of a suit. Thus, legal factors are not likely to be an important factor in encouraging doctors to refer patients to hospice programs.

Do patients in hospice programs have a right to medical care that will prolong their life?

It depends. Terminally ill persons may go through a very long dying process. Some illnesses may cause slow, but steady deterioration over a period of several months. The patient's psychological state will influence the dying process. Medical care can also lengthen the process of dying. Some treatments, such as antibiotics for pneumonia, or resuscitation for cardiac arrest, may enable terminally ill patients to live several days, weeks, or even months, in a state that is meaningful for them and their next of kin. On the other hand, medical treatment may merely prolong dying, be highly intrusive, and keep the patient from a dignified death. An important unresolved issue of hospice care is how to handle this possible conflict between palliative and curative care.

The hospice is designed to provide palliative care for terminally ill patients, and may lack the technology available in hospitals to resuscitate patients or provide intensive care. As a result of this philosophy, hospice patients may not receive the medical care available in hospitals to prolong their life. Patients who enter hospice programs, therefore, should not assume that medical treatment will be provided. Hospices will vary in the range of medical, nonpalliative treatment that they offer. In some cases, the patient's own physician is expected to provide care. Others will treat certain symptoms but do nothing about cardiac arrest, hemorrhage, pneumonia, or the inability to eat solid food.

The patient's right to receive treatment in a hospice program will depend on the patient's knowledge of, and free consent to, the limitations on medical care that it entails. Patients who do not freely consent, would have a right to receive medical care that could extend their life in a meaningful way since a doctor-patient relationship, and hence a duty to protect the interests of the patient, will usually exist.

To assure that patients are fully informed and freely consent to the arrangements involved, the hospice should disclose its policies regarding life-prolonging care. Patients should know in advance whether treatment will be provided for pneumonia, cardiac arrest, hemorrhage, and other developments, even though such treatment will not reverse the patient's underlying illness. Given the hospice's philosophy of candor, such disclosure should not pose a problem.

Must hospices inform patients that they are dying?

Probably. Most hospice patients will be aware of their situation. They will understand the meaning of hospice care and will have freely chosen to forego more aggressive medical treatment that could extend their life. A few patients, however, may not be fully aware of their situation and not realize that hospice care does not provide the life-prolonging medical treatment that they would want. These patients may want aggressive treatment, at least for such conditions as pneumonia, cardiac arrest, and hemorrhage. To make an informed choice, these patients will need a realistic appraisal of their chances for survival. Hospices should thus assure that patients are fully informed of their prognosis and the limits of hospice care, so that they are not denied medical care that they want.

Is hospice care covered by health insurance?

At the present time only Connecticut[6] has passed legislation requiring that health insurance policies also cover special social services for the terminally ill that would include hospice programs. As patient demand for hospice services grow, other states are likely to pass similar laws in the future.

Without laws requiring insurance coverage of hospice services, a person's right to have hospice care covered, depends on the scope of the coverage of the insurance policy or contract that the patient has entered into with the insurer. If it does not offer coverage of home care or inpatient hospice services, a patient does not have a right to reimbursement or payment for these services. However, it is likely that some health insurers will begin to provide coverage for hospice services, since such programs are usually cheaper than the inpatient hospital care they would otherwise receive. As patient demand for hospice services grows and their benefits, including cost-effectiveness, becomes clear, health insurance may begin to include it in its coverage.

Is hospice care covered by Medicare?

Yes. Starting on November 1, 1983 hospice care for the dying will be available under Medicare to patients who meet eligibility requirements, and who have access to a hospice program meeting certain minimum standards.[7] To be eligible for reimbursement a hospice program must provide certain core services, including physician and nursing care, medical social services, pastoral counseling, and family bereavement counseling, but it may use other community agencies to furnish short term in-patient care, homemaker care, occupational, physical and speech therapy, and medical supplies and drugs. The program must also conform to any applicable state licensure laws.

Patients qualify for reimbursement if they have been certified as terminally ill by a physician within six months prior to entering the program. Benefits are available for two 90-day periods and one thirty-day period, though patients will be reimbursed for only 40 percent of total cost of the 210 days of hospice care covered. In practice patients will find most of their expenses covered, since patients use hospice programs for 45 to 50 days on the average. There is also a 5% copayment requirement for out-patient drugs and in-patient "respite" care which is offered to provide a break period for family members.

Must hospice facilities be licensed by the state?

It depends on the state and the characterization of the facility under state law. In some states, hospices would be considered intermediate care facilities or nursing homes, and licensing requirements for such facilities, including staffing, safety, space, and sanitation requirements, would have to be met. As hospice programs grow, separate licensing requirements for hospices are likely to be enacted. This will serve to protect hospice patients from abuse or exploitation without burdensome requirements more suitable for other types of health facilities. At the present time some form of licensure now exists in Connecticut, Florida, Michigan, Nevada and Virginia, with legislation pending in six other states.

NOTES

1. Stoddard, *The Hospice Movement*, 167–69 (1978); Holden, *Hospices: For the Dying, Relief From Pain and Fear*, 193 Science 389–90 (1976).
2. Krant, *The Hospice Movement*, 299 N. Eng. J. Med. 546, 547 (1978).
3. *Id.* at 546.
4. *Id.* at 547.
5. *Id.* at 548.
6. Connecticut Public Act 78–76.
7. Tax Equity and Fiscal Responsibility Act of 1982, Pub.L.No. 97–248. U.S. CODE CONG. & AD. NEWS 3, 35–45 (Sept. 1982).

Appendix A

Organizations Involved with Legal Rights of the Critically Ill

Alliance for Cannabis
  Therapeutics (ACT)
P.O. Box 23691
Washington, DC 20024
(202) 544–2884

American Civil Liberties
  Union
132 West 43 Street
New York, NY 10036
(212) 944–9800

American Society of Law and
  Medicine
Suite 211
520 Commonwealth Avenue
Boston, MA 02215
(617) 262–4990

Americans United for Life
230 N. Michigan Ave., Suite
  915
Chicago, IL 60601
(312) 263–5029

Committee Against
  Intractable Pain
P.O. Box 34571
Washington, DC 20034
(301) 983–1710

Concern for Dying
250 West 57 Street
New York, NY 10019
(212) 246–6962

Institute of Society, Ethics and
  the Life Sciences (Hastings
  Institute)
360 Broadway
Hastings-on-Hudson, NY
  10706
(914) 478–0500

National Health Law Program
2401 Main Street
Santa Monica, CA 90405
(213) 392–4811

National Hospice Organization
1311–A Dolly Madison
Boulevard
Suite 3–B
McLean, VA 22101
(703) 356–6770

National Senior Citizens Law
  Center
1709 West 8 Street
Los Angeles, CA
(213) 483–3990

161

Society for the Right to Die
250 West 57 Street
New York, NY 10019
(212) 246–6973

The Joseph and Rose
    Kennedy Institute of Ethics
    Center for Bioethics
Georgetown University
Washington, DC 20057
(202) 625–2371

Appendix B

States With Laws Allowing Therapeutic Use of Laetrile and Marijuana

(For a description of these laws and citations see chapter III)

Marijuana

Alabama
Arizona
California
Colorado
Florida
Georgia
Illinois
Iowa
Louisiana
Maine
Michigan
Minnesota
Montana
Nevada
New Jersey
New Mexico
New York
North Carolina
Ohio
Oregon
Rhode Island
South Carolina
Texas

Virginia
Washington
West Virginia
Wisconsin

Laetrile

Alaska
Arizona
Delaware
Florida
Idaho
Illinois
Indiana
Kansas
Louisiana
Nevada
New Hampshire
New Jersey
Oklahoma
Oregon
Texas
Washington

Appendix C

States with Brain Death Statutes

State	*Citation*
Alabama	Ala. Code §§ 22–31–1 - 22–31–4 (Cum. Supp. 1979)
Alaska	ALASKA STAT. § 90.65–120 (Cum. Supp. 1979)
Arkansas	ARK. STAT. ANN. §§ 82–537 - 82–538 (Cum. Supp. 1981)
California	CAL. HEALTH & SAFETY Code § 7180 (West 1975)
Colorado	COLO. REV. STAT. § 12–36–136 (1981)
Connecticut	CONN. GEN. STAT. § 19–139i(b) as amended by S.B. 694 (Laws 1979)
District of Columbia	D.C. Code § 6–2401 (1981)
Florida	FLA. STAT. ANN. § 382.085 (West Supp. 1980)
Georgia	GA. CODE ANN. § 88.1715.1 (1975)
Hawaii	HAWAII REV. STAT. tit. 19, § 327c–1 (Supp. 1978)
Idaho	IDA. CODE § 54–1819 (1977)
Illinois	ILL. ANN. STAT. ch. 3, § 552(b) (Smith-Hurd Supp.1975)
Iowa	IA. CODE ANN. § 702.8 (West 1976)
Kansas	KAN. STAT. § 77–202, as amended by S.B. 99 (Laws 1979)
Louisiana	LA. REV. STAT. ANN. § 9:111 (West 1976)
Maryland	MD. CODE ANN., Aer. 43, § 54F (1972)
Michigan	MICH. STAT. ANN. § 14.228(2), repealed by MICH. STAT. ANN. § 14.15(1021) to (1024) (1979)
Mississippi	1981 Miss. Laws ch. 410 (1981)

Missouri	H.B.1223, 2nd Reg. Session, 81st General Assembly (1982)
Montana	MONT. REV. CODE ANN. § 50–22–101 (1977)
Nevada	NEV. REV. STAT. § 451, as amended by S.B. 5 (Laws 1979)
New Mexico	N.M. STAT. ANN. § 12–2–4 (1978)
North Carolina	N.C. GEN. STAT. § 90–323, as amended by S.B. 771 (1979)
Ohio	OHIO REV. CODE ANN. § 2108.30 (Baldwin 1982)
Oklahoma	OKLA. STAT. ANN. tit. 63, § 1–301(g) (West. 1975)
Oregon	ORE. REV. STAT. ch. 565, § 1 (1975)
Tennessee	TENN. CODE ANN. § 53–459 (1976) Tennessee Public Laws, ch. 763 (1982)
Texas	TEX. PUB. HEALTH CODE ANN. tit. 71, § 4447t (Vernon Supp. 1979)
Vermont	VT. STAT. ANN. tit. 18, § 5218 (1981)
Virginia	VA. CODE § 54.325.7, as amended by S.B. 661 (Laws 1979)
West Virginia	W. VA. CODE § 16.19–1 (Supp. 1975)
Wisconsin	Wis. Stat. § 146.71 (1982)

Appendix D
States with Living Will Legislation

(For a description of these laws and citations see chapter VIII)

Alabama
Arkansas
California
District of Columbia
Idaho
Kansas

Nevada
New Mexico
North Carolina
Oregon
Texas
Washington

Appendix E
Sample Living Will Forms

Living wills may vary in form and detail. The following are some representative examples that have been used by many people. (See chapter VIII for an analysis of which forms are most likely to be legally binding).

Concern For Dying

TO MY FAMILY, MY PHYSICIAN, MY LAWYER
AND ALL OTHERS WHOM IT MAY CONCERN

Death is as much a reality as birth, growth, maturity and old age—it is the one certainty of life. If the time comes when I can no longer take part in decisions for my own future, let this statement stand as an expression of my wishes and directions, while I am still of sound mind.

If at such a time the situation should arise in which there is no reasonable expectation of my recovery from extreme physical or mental disability, I direct that I be allowed to die and not be kept alive by medications, artificial means or "heroic measures". I do, however, ask that medication be mercifully administered to me to alleviate suffering even though this may shorten my remaining life.

This statement is made after careful consideration and is in accordance with my strong convictions and beliefs. I want the wishes and directions here expressed carried out to the extent permitted by law. Insofar as they are not legally enforceable, I hope that those of whom this Will is addressed will regard themselves as morally bound by these provisions.

Signed _____

Date _____

Witness _____

Witness _____

Copies of this request
   have been given to_____

_____

_____

_____

Society For The Right To Die Model Bill

DECLARATION

Declaration made this _____ day of _____ (month, year).

I, _____, being of sound mind, willfully and voluntarily make known my desire that my dying shall not be artificially prolonged under the circumstances set forth below, do hereby declare:

If at any time I should have an incurable injury, disease, or illness certified to be a terminal condition by two physicians who have personally examined me, one of whom shall be my attending physician, and the physicians have determined that my death will occur whether or not life-sustaining procedures are utilized and where the application of life-sustaining procedures would serve only to artificially prolong the dying process, I direct that such procedures be withheld or withdrawn, and that I be permitted to die naturally with only the administration of medication or the performance of any medical procedure deemed necessary to provide me with comfort care.

In the absence of my ability to give directions regarding the use of such life-sustaining procedures, it is my intention that this declaration shall be honored by my family and physician(s) as the final expression of my legal right to refuse medical or surgical treatment and accept the consequences from such refusal.

I understand the full import of this declaration and I am emotionally and mentally competent to make this declaration.

Signed _____

City, County and State of Residence _____

The declarant has been personally known to me and I believe him or her to be of sound mind.

Witness _____

Witness _____

The California Model

DIRECTIVE TO PHYSICIANS

Directive made this _____ day of _____ (month, year).

I _____, being of sound mind, willfully, and voluntarily make known my desire that my life shall not be artificially prolonged under the circumstances set forth below, do hereby declare:

1. If at any time I should have an incurable injury, disease, or illness certified to be a terminal condition by two physicians, and where the application of life-sustaining procedures would serve only to artificially prolong the moment of my death and where my physician determines that my death is imminent whether or not life-sustaining procedures are utilized, I direct that such procedures be withheld or withdrawn, and that I be permitted to die naturally.

2. In the absence of my ability to give directions regarding the use of such life-sustaining procedures, it

is my intention that this directive shall be honored by my family and physician(s) as the final expression of my legal right to refuse medical or surgical treatment and accept the consequences from such refusal.

3. If I have been diagnosed as pregnant and that diagnosis is known to my physician, this directive shall have no force or effect during the course of my pregnancy.

4. I have been diagnosed and notified at least 14 days ago as having a terminal condition by _____, M.D., whose address is _____, and whose telephone number is _____. I understand that if I have not filled in the physician's name and address, it shall be presumed that I did not have a terminal condition when I made out this directive.

5. This directive shall have no force or effect five years from the date filled in above.

6. I understand the full import of this directive and I am emotionally and mentally competent to make this directive.

Signed _____

City, County and State of Residence _____

The declarant has been personally known to me and I believe him or her to be of sound mind.

Witness _____
Witness _____

Index

JOHN A. ROBERTSON is a Professor of Law at the University of Texas Law School, Austin, Texas, where he teaches Criminal Law, Constitutional Law, and Law and Medicine. A graduate of Dartmouth College and Harvard Law School (1968), he has written extensively on medical-legal and bioethical issues. He has also been a professor at the University of Wisconsin Law School, and in the Program in Medical Ethics of the University of Wisconsin Medical School, Madison, Wisconsin.